Jane
Addams

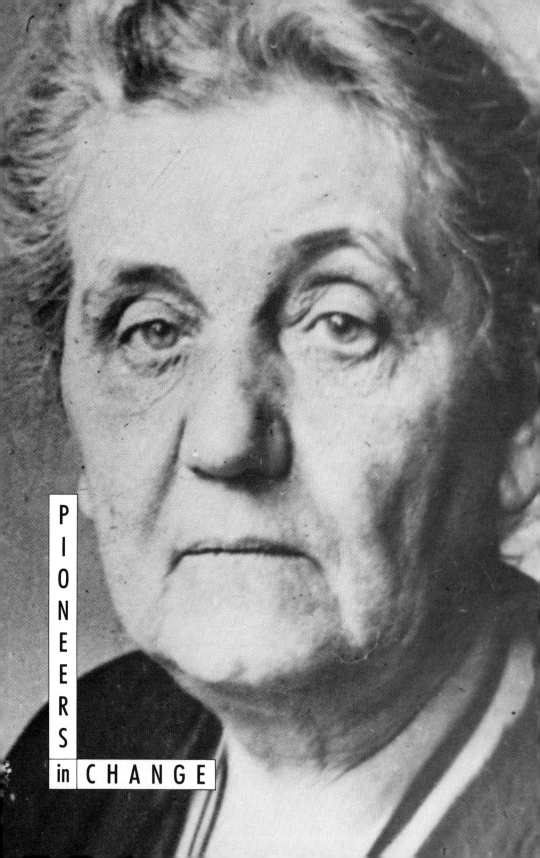

Jane
Addams

LESLIE A. WHEELER

Silver Burdett Press
Englewood Cliffs, New Jersey

For my father, John L. Wheeler
1909–1989

CONSULTANTS

Elizabeth Blackmar, Assistant Professor of History, Columbia College, New York.
Robert M. Goldberg, Department Chairperson, Social Studies, Oceanside Middle
School, Oceanside, New York.

TEXT CREDITS:

From *Jane Addams: A Biography*, by James Weber Linn. Copyright © 1968
Hawthorne Books/E.P. Dutton. From *The Second Twenty Years at Hull House*, by Jane
Addams. Copyright © 1930 Macmillan.

PHOTOGRAPH ACKNOWLEDGMENTS:

The Bettmann Archive: frontispiece, pp. 81, 109, 127; The Chicago Historical Society:
p. 64; Culver Pictures, Inc.: p. 84; University of Illinois at Chicago, The University
Library, Jane Addams Memorial Collection: pp. 3, 7, 9, 36, 40, 45, 51, 123; Women's
International League for Peace and Freedom Papers, Swarthmore College, Peace
Collection: p. 97

SERIES AND COVER
DESIGN:

R STUDIO T Raúl Rodríguez
and Rebecca Tachna

ART DIRECTOR:
Linda Huber

MANAGING EDITOR:
Nancy Furstinger

PROJECT EDITOR:
Richard G. Gallin

PHOTO RESEARCH:
Omni-Photo Communications, Inc.

Published by Silver Burdett Press, Inc., a division of Simon & Schuster, Inc.,
Englewood Cliffs, NJ 07632
Manufactured in the United States of America.
ISBN 0-382-09962-1 (Lib. bdg.)
10 9 8 7 6 5 4 3 2 1
ISBN 0-382-09968-0 (pbk.)
10 9 8 7 6 5 4 3 2 1
Library of Congress Cataloging-in-Publication Data

Wheeler, Leslie, 1945–
Jane Addams / Leslie A. Wheeler.
p.   cm.—(Pioneers in change)
Includes bibliographical references.
Summary: A biography of the wealthy woman who realized her ambition to live and
work among the poor and founded Hull House, one of the first social settlement
houses in the United States.
1. Addams, Jane, 1860–1935—Juvenile literature.   2. Social workers—United States—
Biography—Juvenile literature.   3. Women social reformers—United States—
Biography—Juvenile literature.[1. Addams, Jane, 1860–1935.   2. Social workers.]   I.
Title.   II. Series
HV40.32.A33W44   1990   361.3′.092—dc20
[B]   90-34186
                                                                                            CIP
                                                                                       AC r90

CONTENTS

1

"Jennie"

"Jane Addams of Hull House and the Women's International League for Peace and Freedom"—these words mark the gravestone of an extraordinary woman. Selected by Addams herself, they accurately reflect the two major concerns of her life.

Jane Addams is famous as the founder of Hull House in Chicago, one of the first settlement houses, or centers providing help to poor people living in cities. Her activities in the peace movement are much less well known. During her lifetime, these activities were extremely unpopular. Yet she deserves to be remembered for both her humanitarian and her antiwar work.

Jane Addams was and continues to be a heroine to millions of Americans. But when she herself was growing up, she had only heroes. The men she most admired included the sixteenth president of the United States, Abraham Lincoln; the writer and philosopher Ralph Waldo Emerson; the Italian patriot Giuseppe Mazzini; and her own father.

John Huy Addams was a self-made man who rose to wealth and distinction by his own efforts. Born in Pennsylvania of English Quaker stock, he started out as a miller's apprentice. When he was twenty-two, he married his employer's sister-in-law, Sarah Weber. Sarah, an intelligent young woman who was five years older than John, had attended boarding school in Philadelphia.

After their honeymoon, John Addams and his new bride spent several months traveling around northern Illinois, looking for a place to settle. John was attracted by the opportunities to be had in this still-new country. Also, relatives on both sides had already settled in Illinois. In 1844 he and Sarah made their home at a location on the banks of the Cedar River. It was six miles north of Freeport and within the village of Cedarville, which had only been started nine years before.

John Addams went to work right away. He bought a sawmill and a gristmill. He planted pine trees on the hill across from these with seeds brought all the way from Pennsylvania. He also helped organize the building of a railroad, the Galena and Chicago Union, constructed a large new mill, and took part in establishing a bank, of which he became president. Through hard work and careful planning, he prospered.

John Addams was a leader in local and state affairs. He helped organize Cedarville's first school and first subscription library, in which members paid a fee to belong. He also helped organize its first church. Though he considered himself a Quaker, John Addams never actually joined the

John Addams was an active citizen in his community and an elected lawmaker to the Illinois State Senate for many years.

Society of Friends. Nor did he become an official member of any of the other Protestant churches established in Cedarville and the surrounding area. Instead, he gave generously to all these churches.

In 1854, John Addams was elected to the state senate. He was reelected every two years until 1870, when he decided not to run. In 1854, too, Addams was present at the founding of the Republican party in Wisconsin. He was a friend and admirer of Abraham Lincoln, as well as a strong abolitionist who wanted to end slavery. During the Civil War, he raised and helped equip a company in an Illinois regiment, called after him, "The Addams Guard."

While John Addams built up his business and took part in politics, his wife was busy at home. Along with most women of her time, Sarah Addams believed that her place was in the home, managing the household and taking care of their growing family. She gave birth to nine children. But like many nineteenth-century mothers, she had to bear the sorrow of losing several of her children at very young ages. Only Jane, two older sisters, and an older brother lived to maturity.

Born on September 6, 1860, Jane was the eighth of these nine children. Christened Laura Jane, she was called "Jennie" as a girl. The nickname owed its popularity to the famous Swedish singer, Jenny Lind, who had recently made a very successful tour of the United States.

Jennie Addams was a sickly child. The most serious of her various illnesses was tuberculosis of the spine. It left her with a slight curvature of the back, made her pigeon-toed, and caused her to carry her head cocked to one side.

Jennie's early years were also shadowed by the tragedy of her mother's death. This happened in January 1863 when Jennie was a little over two years old. Pregnant with her ninth child, Sarah Addams went to assist another woman with the delivery of her baby. However, on the way home, Sarah stumbled and fell. Her own baby was born prematurely and died almost immediately. A week later, Sarah followed her newborn to the grave. She was forty-nine years old.

After their mother's death, Jennie's oldest sister, seventeen-year-old Mary, took charge of the household. She had help from a couple of hired girls, a nurse who had been with the family a long time, and the next oldest, thirteen-year-old Martha. Both Mary and Martha pampered young Jennie.

When Jennie was six, however, Martha was suddenly stricken with typhoid fever and died. Jennie was deeply affected by this new loss. She had nightmares in which Mary died and there was no one to love her. After Martha's death, Jennie drew even closer to Mary.

Yet Jennie's "doglike devotion" was reserved for her austere and often absent father. Because he had the flattened thumb of a miller, she spent hours rubbing ground wheat between her thumb and forefinger. Still, she was careful not to be seen walking on the street with her father on Sunday because she didn't want strangers to know that "my handsome father owned this homely little girl."

John Addams had a reputation as an honest, upright man, and young Jennie was determined to live up to his example. On one occasion when she had told a lie, she felt so guilty she couldn't sleep at night. Finally she got out of bed, tiptoed into her father's room, and made her confession. Her father told her that "if he 'had a little girl who told lies,' he was very glad she 'felt too bad to go to sleep afterward.'"

When she did sleep, Jennie was often bothered by a troubling dream. In this dream, everyone in the world except herself was dead and to her fell the responsibility of making a wagon wheel. This was a tremendous responsibility because the affairs of the world couldn't resume until the wheel had been made. Yet as she stood in the deserted blacksmith shop of her dream, she had no idea how to begin. The next morning would find her in the actual village blacksmith shop, silently struggling to memorize as many details of the process as she could.

Around this time, too, Jennie had her first glimpse of real poverty in the back streets of Freeport. She asked her father "why people lived in such horrid little houses so close together." After he had explained, she declared that when she grew up she would live in a large house. However, it wouldn't be surrounded by other big houses, but would stand "in the midst of horrid little houses" like the ones in Freeport.

When Jennie was seven, her father's remarriage brought important changes to her life. Anna Haldeman was an attractive, accomplished woman who wanted to make the Addams household into a cultural and artistic center. An avid reader, she shared her enthusiasm for books with the children. She was also a talented musician. One of the first things she did was to move her piano into the living room. She added other elegant furniture and saw to it that she and her husband entertained often and well.

In addition, the new Mrs. Addams introduced a hitherto unknown degree of discipline into the household. Around the time of her arrival, Jennie's oldest sister, Mary, moved away from home, first to attend Rockford Seminary, then to marry a Presbyterian minister. Her other sister, Alice, also left home to attend Rockford a year later. Jennie had been spoiled by her older sisters. Now she had to adjust to a more strict routine. Another problem was her stepmother's frequent outbursts of temper.

Yet as time went on, Jennie and her new "Ma" grew fond of each other. Under Mrs. Addams's guidance, Jennie developed a new confidence in social situations and an appreciation for culture that remained with her all her life.

Jennie's stepmother was a widow with two children of her own. When she moved into the Addamses' two-story,

*Jane Addams's home was in Cedarville, Illinois. Anna Haldeman
Addams is on the balcony.*

gray-brick house, they did, too. Harry Haldeman was eigh-
teen when his mother remarried. He was outgoing, independent, and highly intelligent. The other son, George, was
seven and only six months younger than Jennie. Quick-
witted, imaginative, and adventurous, George helped bring
quiet, inward-looking Jennie out of herself. The two children soon became inseparable.

Together they roamed the countryside around Cedarville, climbing hills, exploring caves, and wandering in the woods. George was keenly interested in the study of nature. Jennie learned to share this interest, too. Inspired by George's example, she began to dream of becoming a scientist or a doctor herself.

Along with the other children of the village, Jennie and George went to a one-room school. Jennie's favorite subjects were Latin and English. She was not a good speller, but she loved to read and was a leader in the school literary society.

Jennie's father encouraged her in her reading. He himself read a great deal. The subscription library he had helped to start was located in the Addamses' house. He even bribed Jennie by offering her five cents for every volume of the biographies of classical heroes in *Plutarch's Lives* she completed and twenty-five cents for every volume of Washington Irving's *Life of Washington*. Without being bribed, Jennie read Louisa May Alcott's *Little Women* over and over again.

Jennie's father inspired her ambition and sense of purpose. He taught her the importance of hard work and achievement. Yet there were limits to what he expected her to accomplish. John Addams believed in education for women so they could become better wives and mothers, but not doctors or scientists. This difference between her family's expectations and her own ambitions would eventually become a source of much conflict for Jennie.

Meanwhile, she was developing into a slim, attractive young woman. She wore her brown hair pulled back in a bun and liked pretty dresses. Although her dark eyes gave her a look of sadness, she was capable of laughter—even at herself.

*Jane Addams at about age sixteen, with Anna Haldeman Addams
and George Haldeman.*

Overall, Jennie enjoyed a relatively happy childhood. True, she was sickly, but rather than dwelling on her illnesses, she silently endured them. True also, her home life had been darkened by tragedy and was sometimes marred by conflict. Nevertheless, the various family members managed to remain close.

The village of Cedarville was itself a stable community. Some families like the Addamses were wealthy, while others were poor. Yet they shared a common Protestant religion and Yankee, or New England, heritage.

Jennie felt great affection for both her hometown and her family. But by the time she was seventeen, she was ready to leave this secure environment for the wider world of college.

2

At Rockford Seminary

In September 1877, Jane Addams entered the Rockford Female Seminary as a first-year student. The seminary was located in Rockford, Illinois, a fair-sized factory town that was only thirty miles away from Cedarville. Jane went there reluctantly, because Rockford was known for its intensely religious atmosphere. She herself was not a member of any church. Nor had she even been baptized. Also, she wanted to earn a college degree, and Rockford did not offer one. Graduates received certificates rather than college degrees.

Jane had her heart set on going to Smith College in the East. She had even taken and passed the examinations for Smith. But her father did not want her to be so far from home. Besides, he was on the board of trustees, or directors, of Rockford, and Jane's two older sisters had gone there.

Still, Jane thought of herself as a college woman and

therefore a pioneer. Her generation of women was the first for whom a college education was a real possibility. Before the Civil War, a few girls had attended Mount Holyoke Female Seminary, Oberlin College, or one of a handful of other colleges. But the education they received at these places was equivalent to a high school rather than a college education. The years after the Civil War saw the founding of the first real women's colleges—Vassar in 1861, Smith in 1872, Wellesley in 1875.

Congregational and Presbyterian ministers had established Rockford in 1847. It was modeled after Mount Holyoke, which had been founded ten years earlier. Rockford was often referred to as the "Mount Holyoke of the West." Like Mount Holyoke, Rockford's purpose was to send out educated, Christian women into various fields of usefulness.

The seminary's principal, Anna Peck Sill, was a deeply religious New Englander who had wanted to be a missionary. She made sure that the missionary spirit prevailed at Rockford. All students were required to attend daily chapel, weekly prayer meetings, church on Sunday morning, and Sunday school in the afternoon. There were also monthly days for fasting, an annual prayer week in January, and in the evenings throughout the school year, informal prayer meetings between the two study periods.

As at Mount Holyoke, life at Rockford was highly regimented. The rising bell rang at 6:30 every morning. Breakfast was served promptly at seven o'clock. A faculty member sat at the head of every table in the dining hall. No one could sit down until Miss Sill gave the signal. Those who misbehaved received bad marks against their names. Some were even expelled.

Every student had to keep an account book. Teachers inspected these books every week. They cautioned against extravagance and scolded girls who wore expensive clothes or elaborate jewelry. Only seniors were allowed to go to downtown Rockford without a chaperone.

All students also had to supply their own sheets, blankets, napkins, and tableware for meals. They were supposed to tend the wood-burning stoves in their rooms, sweep the floors, and carry their own wash water. In addition, an hour of "domestic work" was required each day. Tasks included setting and clearing tables, washing glasses and silver, making pies and cakes, answering the door bell, sorting mail, and straightening up the classrooms. In this way, Rockford, like Mount Holyoke, provided instruction in household chores—and kept costs down. (The yearly charge for room, board, and tuition was $175.)

At Rockford, Jane joined a student body of nearly two hundred students. There were twenty-some students in her own class of 1881. But a half dozen dropped out before graduation. Jane's classmates were the daughters of farmers, ministers, or owners of small businesses. Only a few came from wealthy families.

Like Jane, most of these young women saw themselves as college women. Following the example of their counterparts elsewhere, the Class of '81 composed a class song and designed their own class stationery. It featured a picture of hops and wheat and the class motto, *blaefdige*, the Anglo-Saxon word for lady, which meant "bread-giver" in translation.

Jane was homesick in the beginning. But she soon made friends and settled into the routine of life at Rockford. In Latin class, she met Ellen Gates Starr. Ellen came from

Durand, Illinois, a small country town nearby. There her father was engaged in business. A slight girl with an intense nature, a ready wit, and a deep interest in art, she and Jane became close friends. Ellen left Rockford after a year to become a schoolteacher. But she and Jane kept in touch by means of long, intimate letters.

Theirs was a very intellectual friendship, for in their letters, Jane and Ellen discussed books they had read, lectures attended, and new ideas being put forward. It was also a sentimental and romantic friendship, in which the two girls addressed each other as "Dear One" and celebrated September 11, the day they had first met, even after they were apart. Such attachments were common among young women in the nineteenth century.

Jane was also very popular with the other students. Her room on the second floor of ivy-covered Linden Hall was a favorite gathering place. Many tried to become her confidante, wanted her picture, or begged her to write them. Nevertheless, Jane held herself somewhat aloof. Her manner was always a bit more formal than that of the other girls. For example, she preferred "Miss Addams" to "Jane." All the girls were addressed as "Miss" in class. But Jane was one of the few who insisted on this form of address outside of class.

Jane had her share of admirers among the young men as well. Beloit College was just a few miles away, and romances often blossomed between the Beloit boys and the Rockford girls. One of Jane's admirers at Beloit was a young man named Rollin Salisbury. Another was her stepbrother, George Haldeman. Her sister Alice had fallen in love with and married Harry Haldeman. Yet Jane wasn't romantically interested in George or the other young man.

The Rockford girls could have male visitors only on

Saturdays. The rest of the week they were busy with their studies. Jane did extremely well at Rockford. She studied German and Latin, astronomy, botany, and geology, medieval history, civil government, geography, and American literature. She also had to study the Bible and take a few other courses that reflected Rockford's strong religious orientation.

Jane and some of the other students pressed for courses that would help them qualify for a college degree. She and another student studied higher mathematics for this reason. Jane was also one of the few who studied Greek. A high point of her educational experience was her study of the poet Homer in the original Greek.

For the special program her class put on in their junior year, Jane made a speech about a hero of Greek myths, Bellerophon. Mounted on a winged horse, Pegasus, Bellerophon slew a monster called the Chimera. Jane worked for weeks on this speech. A copy then went to the Greek professor at Beloit College, who checked it for mistakes. In the speech, Jane declared that social evils could only be overcome by people who soared idealistically above them, like Bellerophon on his winged horse. Her oration was a great success. But because it was all in Greek, her classmates couldn't understand a word.

Jane was also keenly interested in science. Her interest stemmed in part from her two stepbrothers. After studying medicine in Germany, Harry Haldeman had become a doctor. George liked to conduct simple scientific experiments. In her freshman year, Jane helped found a scientific society at Rockford. Then during the summer after her sophomore year, she and George studied comparative anatomy together. Back at Rockford, she was thrilled by the opportunity to dissect and stuff a hawk.

Along with her stepbrothers and some of her classmates, Jane was excited by the theory of evolution. The English naturalist Charles Darwin's book, *The Origin of Species*, had caused a huge stir when it was published about twenty years before. Darwin argued that all life had evolved, or developed from simpler forms of life. His theory of how life developed offended many religious people, because they felt it went against the teachings of the Bible. When Jane returned to Rockford after a vacation spent reading two of Darwin's books that belonged to her stepbrother Harry, her classmates marveled at her daring.

Another book that had a big impact on Jane and her classmates was *Dreams* by an Englishman named Thomas De Quincey. De Quincey had experimented with the drug opium. Opium was not an illegal drug at that time. In fact, it was commonly used in many patent medicines to help people sleep or to relieve pain. Jane and four friends were fascinated by the experiences De Quincey had while under the influence of opium. They decided to try the drug themselves. They took small doses at intervals over a long holiday. But the excitement and suspense kept them from falling asleep and having any of the fantastic dreams De Quincey described.

The experiment ended abruptly when a young teacher they had taken into their confidence became alarmed. She took away their De Quincey and the rest of the opium powders. She sent them to their rooms with orders to appear at family worship, whether or not they felt up to it. Thus ended Jane's experiments with dangerous drugs.

Jane was very interested in literature and writing as well as science. Two of her favorite authors were the Scotsman Thomas Carlyle and the Englishman John Ruskin. Both writers stressed the need for the individual to do his or her duty in order to reform, that is, change and improve, society.

Jane also took part in debates, was elected president of the Literary Society, and contributed to the *Rockford Seminary Magazine*. This magazine was published "in the interest of the Seminary and the cause of Christian education in general." But during Jane's junior year, she and a few others worked to change the magazine so that it spoke more to the actual concerns of Rockford students.

Already Jane thought of herself as a writer. She slaved over the essays she wrote for the college magazine and over her college themes, or written exercises. She saved these essays and themes, reworked them, and in time, used some of the ideas in her later writings. With titles like "The Element of Hopefulness in Human Nature," the essays reveal her strong idealism. She had no desire to write fiction, which she thought frivolous. Instead, she wanted to write about what she considered important subjects.

Like many of the first generation of college women, Jane was a feminist. However, she was not so much concerned with the issue of women's getting the vote as with their role in the world. In an essay entitled "Breadgivers," Jane wrote that the young women of her generation did not wish to be men or like men but that they claimed "the same right to independent thought and action." At the same time, she asserted they clung to the old ideal of womanhood. This she defined as that of "the Saxon lady whose mission it was to give bread unto her household."

Jane's words broke with the traditional view of women's

role. Instead of remaining passive, she wanted women to be active providers or "breadgivers." A woman could be a "breadgiver" as a wife, mother, and homemaker. But Jane suggested there were other ways women could do this.

In her senior year, Jane had an opportunity to get out into the world beyond Rockford. She and another editor of the college magazine were invited to attend the Interstate Oratorical Contest in Jacksonville, Illinois, and a meeting of college magazine editors

Legend has it that Jane competed in this contest against William Jennings Bryan, later famous as the silver-tongued orator of the Democratic party. In fact, Jane went as an observer. And Bryan himself didn't speak, having lost in an earlier contest.

Nevertheless, Jane enjoyed the experience. While in Jacksonville, she and the other college magazine editor took time to visit the state institutions for the blind and for the deaf and dumb. Jane later wrote that these visits made quite an impression on her.

Another highlight of Jane's senior year was a visit to Rockford by the noted author and educator Bronson Alcott. The first-year students were thrilled, because he was the father of Louisa May Alcott, the author of *Little Women*. However, Jane and the other seniors were excited because Alcott had been a friend of one of their heroes, the writer and philosopher Ralph Waldo Emerson.

Also during her senior year, Jane was pressed to join the Congregational or Presbyterian church and go to Turkey as a missionary. Rockford's head, Anna Sill, was proud of the fact that many of the seminary students had gone forth as missionaries. Several of Jane's classmates actually did answer the call. One started a school in Japan with her missionary husband. Another served as a medical missionary and physician to the royal family in Korea.

Jane, however, steadfastly resisted this pressure. Throughout her four years at Rockford, every effort had been made to get her to become a church member. She and the other students who weren't church members were the subject of prayer at the daily chapel exercise and the weekly prayer meeting. A teacher whom Jane was especially fond of also came to talk to her about religion during silent study hours.

Still, Jane held her ground. She didn't believe that church membership was necessary to believe in God and lead a good life. Her father didn't belong to any church, and he was as upright as any person. Later, she wrote that "this passive resistance of mine, this clinging to individual conviction" was some of the best training she received at Rockford. She learned to stand on her own feet and think for herself.

Although Jane didn't respond to the foreign missionary appeal, she was fired with the ideal of serving humanity. As senior year drew to a close, Jane and her classmates had long, earnest discussions about what they would do when they left Rockford. According to Jane: "It was quite settled in my mind that I would study medicine and 'live with the poor.'"

Jane set forth her ideas about women's special mission in the valedictory, or farewell address, she gave at graduation. The title of her speech was "Cassandra." Cassandra was a Trojan prophetess whose tragedy it was "always to be in the right, always to be disbelieved and rejected."

In ringing tones, Jane drew a parallel between Cassandra's gift of prophecy and womanly intuition. She went on to say that unfortunately women didn't use their intuition properly. As a remedy, Jane suggested that women ought to study at least one branch of physical science. The study of science would help them determine whether their intuition was genuine or not. This done, women would be able to use their "growing insight" to tackle social problems, and might "yet transform the world."

Jane left Rockford Seminary stronger and more sure of herself than before. She had developed her abilities as a writer and a public speaker. She had also proved herself a leader, having been elected class president in both her junior and senior years. She had even won a major victory: Thanks in part to her efforts, Rockford was going to offer its first college degrees. A year after graduation, she returned to receive the coveted degree.

Finally, Jane's four years at Rockford had strengthened her early resolve to do something important with her life. Her immediate plans were to enroll at Smith College in the fall, earn a degree, then travel in Europe before entering medical school. And after that? As she left the platform in triumph on graduation day, Jane Addams may well have felt that almost anything was possible for her.

3

Adrift

The buoyant self-assurance Jane Addams felt at graduation soon gave way to ill health and depression. For the next several years, she was, by her own account, "absolutely at sea so far as any moral purpose was concerned, clinging only to the desire to live in a really living world...."

Jane Addams had not had health problems while at Rockford. But she became ill shortly after her return to Cedarville in the summer of 1881. Her illness didn't surprise her family because she had been ill before. They also weren't surprised because in those days young women weren't supposed to be capable of great mental or physical labor. Doctors of the time regularly cautioned that such exertion would lead to physical and mental breakdown. Little wonder then that many other college women besides Jane Addams had breakdowns. They were merely doing what their families and society as a whole expected of them.

In Addams's case, her illness made her decide to give up her plan to enroll at Smith College in the fall. This pleased her father and stepmother. They had never wanted Jane to go to Smith in the first place. Both were just as glad to have their youngest daughter at home, where they could look after her.

The summer was a trying time for Addams for other reasons as well. On July 2, Charles Julius Guiteau fatally shot President James Garfield in a fit of insanity. Guiteau was the stepbrother of Flora Guiteau, Addams's best friend in the Freeport-Centerville area. Flora's father worked at John Addams's bank, and the girl herself had been a frequent visitor at the Addams house. After the assassination, newspaper reporters flocked to Freeport, hounding Flora and her family. Jane sympathized very much with her friend during this terrible ordeal.

In August, Addams accompanied her father and stepmother on a combined business and pleasure trip to northern Wisconsin. In the midst of inspecting some mining property there, John Addams suddenly became ill. Jane and her stepmother managed to get him to a hospital in Green Bay. But within thirty-six hours he was dead of a burst appendix, or "inflammation of the bowels," as it was then called. John Addams was only fifty-nine when he died.

Her father's death deeply affected Addams. In a letter to Ellen Starr, she described it as "the greatest sorrow that can ever come to me," adding that she hoped in time to regain her sense of purpose. Ellen replied that she would never be disappointed in Jane, because she was too much like her father to let even the greatest sorrow throw her permanently off course.

Ellen Starr was right. Addams soon rallied. In September, she enrolled at the Women's Medical School in Phila-delphia. Why she decided to go to medical school when she hadn't felt well enough to attend Smith isn't clear. Perhaps she wanted to see if she was really up to the challenge of medical studies. She may also have been influenced by her stepmother. Now a widow for the second time, Mrs. Addams didn't look forward to spending the winter in sleepy little Cedarville.

Jane Addams, however, quickly discovered that medical studies didn't particularly interest her. She did well on her examinations, but her heart wasn't in it. She also found herself torn between the need to study and the demands of her stepmother, who wanted her to share in social and cultural activities. Later Addams remembered that her chief difficulty in Philadelphia was trying to do too many things at once.

Before long, she was ill again, and by February, she had abandoned her studies completely. Seeking a cure, she entered S. Weir Mitchell's Hospital of Orthopedic and Nervous Diseases. Weir treated many women who, like Addams, suffered from physical or mental breakdowns and a variety of other complaints. He prescribed complete rest with no visitors, books, or papers.

Weir's rest cure helped Addams's back problems, but she didn't like the enforced inactivity at all. By April she was well enough to return to Cedarville, but she had another breakdown a few months later. Family and friends finally convinced her that her trouble was mostly physical. If her back problem were corrected, she would recover her sense of purpose and drive.

The following fall, Addams went to Mitchelville, Iowa, where her stepbrother, Harry Haldeman, now a skilled surgeon, performed an operation to correct the curvature of her spine. For the next six months, she had to lie flat on her back in bed. When she was finally allowed to get up, her stepbrother fitted her with an elaborate straitjacket made of leather, steel, and whalebone to support her spine.

In the spring, Addams returned to Cedarville where a family crisis awaited her. Weber, her older brother, now married with a family, had a mental breakdown. Jane was the one who had to comfort his wife and also handle most of the financial arrangements.

Besides looking after her brother's affairs, Addams had money and property of her own to manage. Her father's death had left her a wealthy young woman. She had inherited a large farm, stocks, bonds, and other property worth between $50,000 and $60,000. That was a huge amount of money—equal to about $500,000 to $600,000 today. Occasionally Addams complained of having to spend so much time on business matters. But the activity made her feel much better. Late that summer, she decided to follow through with her plan of visiting Europe, as her sisters had done.

In August 1883, Addams set sail with a party that included her stepmother, two college friends, Mary and "Puss" Ellwood, their aunt, and Sarah Anderson, a teacher and friend from Rockford. The famous novelist Henry James also happened to be on board. Between courses at meals, Addams had a chance to study him. She decided that although he looked very English, he didn't appear "especially keen or intellectual."

If Henry James noticed Jane Addams at all, he probably thought her representative of a type he often wrote about in his books. This was the well-to-do young American woman, for whom a trip to Europe was considered the finishing touch to her education before she married and began raising a family.

Addams, however, was determined to be more than a casual sightseer. Her plan was to study the art, language, literature, and history of Europe with the same thoroughness she had brought to her studies at Rockford. Then she meant to do something useful with the knowledge she had gained.

Throughout the two years she and her party spent traveling around England, Holland, Germany, France, Austria, Italy, and Switzerland, Addams kept several notebooks. She also wrote long letters to her sisters and other family members. In these, she faithfully recorded her impressions of cathedrals and museums visited, of concerts and operas attended, and of the universities and literary landmarks at which she stopped.

Addams also set down her reactions to the poverty she saw in Europe. In the slums of London's East End, she caught only a superficial glimpse of "misery and wretchedness." Still, it was enough to make her "thoroughly sad & perplexed."

Later, traveling in Bavaria, in Germany, she praised the beautiful scenery. Yet she was appalled at the conditions under which some of the people lived. In Coburg, for example, she observed a dozen women carrying large casks of hot beer on their backs to a cooling house. The beer sloshed in the containers, spilling and often scalding the heads and shoulders of the women as they walked. Addams further noted that these women worked at this difficult job from five in the morning until seven at night for a mark and a half, or about 37 1/2 cents.

For the most part, Addams enjoyed good health and spirits during the time she spent in Europe. But she failed to recapture the strong sense of purpose that had fired her when she left Rockford. Thus, as she confessed to Ellen Starr, her European travels almost seemed a waste of time.

The two years following her return from Europe in the summer of 1885 were filled with more anguished searching. Addams had tried both medical school and European travel, and still hadn't found useful work. She was often frustrated and unhappy but continued her quest all the same. She had a vague idea that her future occupation was connected with art and European culture. She wrote articles about her European experiences and studied her notebooks and the art books she had brought back with her.

In the fall of 1885, Jane accompanied her stepmother Anna to Baltimore, Maryland. George Haldeman was working for an advanced degree in science at the new Johns Hopkins University, and his mother wanted to be close to him. Also, Baltimore offered Anna Addams more in the way of social life than Cedarville or Freeport.

Anna Addams did her best to "launch" Jane into Baltimore society. At her stepmother's urging, she attended fashionable parties, concerts, and lectures but took little pleasure in these activities. What she really enjoyed were the visits she paid to some of the city's charitable institutions. These included a sewing school for poor children, a home for elderly black women, and an asylum for black orphans. While lectures or parties wore her out, Jane Addams always perked up after a visit to a charitable institution.

She wasn't pleased, though, by her stepmother's efforts to promote a match between George Haldeman and herself. Although George was romantically interested in her, Jane still thought of him as a brother. She also felt he was misdirecting his energies in the single-minded pursuit of science. For his part, George was impatient with Jane's concern for social problems. Finally, along with most college women of her generation, Addams felt she couldn't combine marriage with a career. And despite the fact she hadn't yet found it, a career was what she most wanted.

Eventually, George had a nervous breakdown, from which he never fully recovered. Anna Addams blamed Jane for her son's illness. Many years afterward, Addams told friends who believed it was possible to receive messages from the spirit world that the only such messages she had received were from her stepmother. In them, Mrs. Addams constantly scolded her for not having married George Haldeman.

All in all, it was a trying time for everyone involved. Addams later wrote that during her stay in Baltimore she reached "the nadir [low point] of my nervous depression."

During the second winter she spent in Baltimore, Addams helped organize an art club of six women. Members attended lectures and exhibits and wrote essays on topics of special interest. She also took drawing lessons. But neither of these activities provided the fulfillment she craved.

Still groping her way toward a worthwhile vocation, Addams decided to make a second trip to Europe. One purpose of the trip was to help Ellen Starr collect art reproductions in Spain and Italy for Rockford College and for the school where Ellen was teaching. Addams offered to pay half of Ellen's traveling expenses, and those of Sarah Anderson, the teacher and friend from Rockford who had accompanied Addams on her first trip to Europe. With an annual income of $3,000 from her property and investments, Addams could afford to be generous. Ellen Starr was so eager to get to Europe that she left in the fall. Addams and Sarah Anderson followed in December 1887.

This second European trip proved to be very different from the first. On the earlier trip, Addams had been called "Mademoiselle" and "Fraulein" and treated like a young girl. Now she was called "Madame" and felt dignified and truly grown-up.

Gone, too, was the pressure to see everything and cram her brain with information. As a result, Addams discovered that she was enjoying her visits to museums and cathedrals more. She was particularly impressed by the cathedral at Ulm in Germany. To her, this soaring edifice with its magnificent stone carvings and stained glass seemed to sum up the history of humanity's spiritual quest.

In Germany, Addams met up with Ellen Starr, and together they traveled to Italy, where Sarah Anderson later joined them. In Rome, Ellen planned to study paintings, and Jane, the catacombs and the history of the early Christians, buried in these underground chambers. Addams had to abandon her program of study, however, when she was stricken by an attack of sciatic rheumatism. This illness knotted one of her legs with pain and confined her to bed for weeks.

Although she didn't feel well enough to accompany them, Addams insisted that Starr and Anderson go to Naples and southern Italy in the spring, as planned. When she was able to travel, Addams went to the Riviera, a resort area along the Mediterranean coast. There she regained her health and strength and was then able to journey to Spain with her friends.

In Madrid, the three young women attended a bull-fight. Addams was fascinated by the spectacle, by the beauty and grace of the bulls, as well as by the skill of the bullfighters. Yet she felt guilty about enjoying such a cruel sport. Later, she remembered the bullfight as a very powerful and troubling experience.

In June 1888, Addams decided to go to London to attend the International Congress of Protestant Missions. Although she had rejected the appeal to become a missionary at Rockford, Addams was still interested in various humanitarian efforts. Perhaps at the conference she would learn something that would help her in her search for useful work. As it turned out, Addams found what she was looking for not at the conference but at Toynbee Hall in London.

Founded four years before by a group of Oxford University men, Toynbee Hall was the first settlement house, a center serving the urban poor. The university men who lived at Toynbee Hall taught classes and helped organize clubs and recreational activities for the working people of East London, where the settlement was located. Although they lived among the poor, Toynbee Hall residents didn't live *like* them. Instead, they enjoyed the same upper-class lifestyle they would have if they had remained at Oxford.

The educational goals of Toynbee Hall appealed to Addams, as did its emphasis on art and culture. Here was a way of helping the poor while at the same time using her knowledge of art and culture. Also, she could continue to live in her customary manner.

Toynbee Hall wasn't the only influence on Addams. She also visited the People's Palace, a philanthropic institution founded the year before. It housed meeting rooms, workshops, and club rooms for working-class people.

In addition, Addams read two novels, *The Children of Gideon* and *Conditions of Men* by the English author Walter

Besant. In both novels, a wealthy young woman decides to live among the poor. One of the heroines even builds a cultural center in the middle of the slums. The People's Palace was based on the plan described in this novel.

Thus in London in June 1888, Addams's seven-year search for something important to do with her life ended. Now she had only to return to the United States and act on her plan.

4

"A Place for Invalid Girls to Go and Help the Poor"

J ane Addams came back from Europe, eager to begin her new life. One of the first things she did was join a church. In the fall of 1888, not long after her twenty-eighth birthday, she was baptized at the Presbyterian Church at Cedarville. About a year later, she was admitted as a member in full standing. Addams may have decided to join a church at this time, because she saw the work she was about to undertake in a religious way. She would serve as a kind of missionary to the poor.

Addams's family didn't object to her joining a church. But they hardly approved of her plan to move to Chicago and start a settlement house in a poor section of the city. They wanted her to go on ministering to family members who needed help. Addams herself was torn between the demands of her family and her own wishes.

Fortunately, Ellen Starr came to Addams's aid at this

critical moment. When Jane had confided her plan to Ellen the previous summer, Ellen had supported her enthusiastically. Now Ellen's friendship and support helped give Jane the courage she needed to break away from her family and strike out on her own.

Late in January, Addams and Starr moved to Chicago. In 1889, Chicago was a huge, bustling place. It was the second-largest city in the country.

Three-quarters of Chicago's population was foreign-born. This was a time of massive immigration from abroad. Immigrants from Italy, Russia, Poland, and the Balkan Peninsula poured into cities like Chicago. They lived in run-down neighborhoods and worked in factories for very low wages. Because of their different languages and customs, and their willingness to work at the lowest-paying jobs, immigrants were feared and hated by many native-born Americans. Immigrants were also sometimes blamed for the growing violence that occurred in the labor movement.

In May 1886, three years before Jane Addams and Ellen Starr arrived in Chicago, workers at the McCormick farm machinery factory went on strike. The company hired men called strikebreakers to keep production going. When workers clashed with these strikebreakers, the Chicago police opened fire, killing four workers.

The next day, thousands of workers gathered in Haymarket Square to protest the shootings and to push for an eight-hour workday. Anarchists—people opposed to organized government—made speeches at the meeting. Still, it was about to break up peacefully when police arrived and ordered the crowd to disperse. Just then a bomb exploded, killing seven policemen. The police fired into the crowd and killed four workers.

To this day, no one knows who set the bomb. Nevertheless, city officials arrested eight labor leaders who were anarchists. Although there was no evidence linking these men to the bombing, they were found guilty of murder and sentenced to death. Four were hanged, one committed suicide, and three were later pardoned by the governor.

The Haymarket Riot left behind much bitterness and resentment. These feelings were directed at the labor movement. They were also directed at immigrants, because anarchist labor leaders were often foreign-born.

In time, Jane Addams and Ellen Starr would have to come to terms with the bitterness and resentment left by the Haymarket Riot. But for the moment, they were too busy getting settled in the city. They took rooms at a lodging house that provided them with their meals. Right away they went to work enlisting the support of various individuals and organizations for their project.

They turned first to the city's churches and missions, or religious organizations involved in humanitarian work. Addams began attending the prestigious Fourth Presbyterian Church. The two young women also met with a number of prominent clergymen. They visited two missions providing various services to poor families.

At one of these, the Armour Mission, they found an enthusiastic supporter in Allen P. Pond, a young architect. He offered to introduce them to others who might be interested and to take them on walking tours of the poor sections of the city, where many immigrants lived.

These walking tours were eye-opening experiences for Addams. For example, on a visit to a German-American neighborhood, she was amazed to find the atmosphere as foreign as she had observed in Germany.

It was the same in an Italian-American neighborhood. Here families spoke nothing but Italian. They dressed like Italian peasants, or small farmers, and were crowded together in a way Addams hadn't thought possible in the United States. She was shocked to discover four families of seven or eight sharing one room, for which they paid eleven dollars a month. Yet she found the people "affectionate and gentle" and not given to begging or complaining. Thus Addams favored settling in an Italian-American neighborhood. Ellen Starr, on the other hand, leaned toward an area with German and French immigrants because more of the college girls they hoped would join them knew these languages.

In her efforts to get to know the city, Addams even visited a Sunday school run by anarchists. Although anarchists were considered extremely dangerous, Addams found their Sunday school to be "very innocent."

When Addams and Starr weren't rubbing elbows with immigrants and anarchists, they were busy attending teas, luncheons, and receptions at the elegant homes and clubs of Chicago's wealthiest and most prominent citizens. Some were people Ellen Starr knew from her days as a teacher at the city's fashionable Kirkland School. Others were acquaintances from Rockford who lived in either the city or nearby suburbs. The young women needed the support of these people for their plan to succeed.

They also contacted groups like the Chicago Women's Club and the local branch of the national organization of women college graduates. One very powerful member of the former club was so impressed with Addams that she promised to get her into the club, even though it took only one member a year.

Another club woman was rushing from one meeting to another, when Addams fell in step with her and began describing her plan. The woman didn't pay much attention until she caught the words "a place for invalid girls to go and help the poor." Turning to stare at her companion for the first time, she was astonished to see "a frail, sensitive girl" who didn't look at all like a reformer. The woman suggested they sit down and talk about the plan, and they did.

When Jane Addams described what she called her "Toynbee Hall experiment," she always stressed the fact that it would serve two purposes. Besides helping the poor, her settlement house would benefit its residents—young, college-educated women, who, lacking an outlet for their talents and abilities, were unhappy and frequently ill.

Having found such an outlet herself, Addams brimmed with high spirits and good health. As Ellen Starr correctly observed, nervous people like her friend didn't need rest but a certain kind of activity. For Addams, this activity included reading all she could about social movements in both Europe and the United States. She quickly discovered that she wasn't the first American to dream of founding a settlement house.

Three years earlier, a young Amherst graduate, Stanton Coit, had visited Toynbee Hall and returned to New York to found the Neighborhood Guild. Vida Scudder, Jean Fine, Helen Rand, and several other graduates of Smith College had also been influenced by Toynbee Hall and Walter Besant's novels. In 1887 they had organized the College Settlement Association. Their group moved into a house on the Lower East Side, a poor immigrant neighborhood in New York City, just a week before Jane Addams and Ellen Starr started their settlement house.

Meanwhile, Addams and Starr continued their search

for a building. That spring, on one of her walking tours with Allen Pond, Addams spotted an old, dilapidated house at the corner of Halstead and Polk streets. She had actually seen the house before on an earlier visit to the neighborhood. But until now, she hadn't been able to find it again.

The Nineteenth Ward, where the house was located, was one of Chicago's worst districts. Its streets were dirty, poorly lit, ill paved, and foul-smelling. Wooden boxes attached to the street pavements were filled to overflowing with garbage and ashes. There were few schools. Although most of the houses had been built for one family, they were now occupied by several. Many had no water supply except for a faucet in the backyard.

The square redbrick structure that caught Jane Addams's eye had once been the mansion of Charles J. Hull, a well-to-do Chicago real estate dealer. Built in 1856 in what was then the suburbs, the house had been swallowed up by the growing city. It was one of the few in the area to survive the Great Chicago Fire of 1871. Now an undertaking establishment stood on one side and a saloon on the other.

The house itself contained a saloon, an office, and a storage room for a nearby furniture company on the first floor. The tenants who occupied the second floor were convinced the attic was haunted. They kept a pitcher of water on the attic stairs on the theory that ghosts wouldn't cross water.

Jane Addams and Ellen Starr immediately contacted the owner, Helen Culver, who was Charles Hull's cousin and secretary. Culver eyed them suspiciously at first. After all, why would two obviously well-bred young ladies want to live in a slum? But through tact and skillful negotiating, the pair brought her around. She agreed to sublet the second floor of

Hull House as it looked at about the time Jane Addams organized it as a settlement house.

the house to them for thirty dollars a month and to give them the use of a large reception room on the first floor.

On September 18, 1889, Addams and Starr moved into Hull House, along with Mary Keyser, a young woman they had hired as a housekeeper. They were proud of their new home and lovingly furnished it with mahogany chairs, oriental rugs, a piano, and art treasures they had collected in Europe. Addams even placed the silver she had inherited in an elegant sideboard. She did so despite warnings from family and friends that all their possessions would be stolen. These same people would have been even more horrified had they known that in the excitement of moving in, Addams and Starr forgot to lock or even close one of the side doors that first night.

If friends and relatives were worried, the young women's new neighbors were baffled by their presence. An elderly Italian-American man shook his head and declared it the strangest thing he had ever seen. Strange or not, Addams and Starr set out to break the ice by inviting several of the young women employees of the furniture factory to dinner followed by a reading party. *Romola*, a novel by the English author George Eliot (whose real name was Marian Evans), was read aloud in Italian.

Addams and Starr chose this novel because it took place in Italy and also because of its plot. Set in medieval Florence, *Romola* tells the story of a young woman whose religious devotion leads her to a life of service among the poor. Addams and Starr also showed their appreciation of Italian culture by laying out on the table stacks of photographs of Florence they had brought back with them.

A variety of activities soon followed the initial reading party. Ellen Starr organized art classes, exhibitions, and a lending library of art reproductions so that their immigrant neighbors could have beautiful pictures to look at. Addams and Starr also provided free lectures on scholarly topics by university professors, college women, and Protestant clergymen. Such programs reflected their belief in the importance of bringing art and culture into the lives of working-class people.

Other programs and services were developed to meet practical needs of the neighborhood. Since many women came to Hull House bringing their children, Addams and Starr decided to start a day nursery and a kindergarten. Jenny Dow, a lively, attractive young woman who came from a prominent Chicago family, volunteered to run the kindergarten and pay all expenses.

Jenny Dow did well with the kindergarten. But she sometimes ran into trouble with the children's immigrant parents because of their different customs. On one occasion, she returned one of her pupils to her home after she decided that the child was intoxicated from a breakfast of bread soaked in wine. The child's Italian-American mother listened politely to Dow's lecture on the evils of drink. Then as a gesture of hospitality, the woman set out her best wines. When her guest refused one after another of the wines, the mother produced a glass of whiskey. "See," she said, beaming, "I have brought you the true American drink."

Addams and Starr also started a boys' club, with Jane taking one section and Ellen the other. Addams had about twenty boys in her group, all about sixteen years old. On the whole, they were an eager, respectful bunch. Yet they had a few bad habits, such as wearing their hats indoors and spitting on the floor.

Sometimes hardly any one showed up for a planned

event. At other times, people simply dropped by. That first year, Hull House had 50,000 visitors. Some came because they were curious; others, because in the crowded West Side of Chicago, there were few places where people could sit and talk with their friends.

Not all visitors were exactly welcome. Twice Jane Addams awoke to find a burglar in her room. The first time, her main concern was not to waken her small nephew who was asleep in the next room. She told the burglar not to make a sound. Then as the startled man made for the window by which he had entered, she cautioned him not to go that way, because he would be hurt. Instead, she told him to use the stairs and let himself out. The burglar did.

The second time, Addams engaged the would-be burglar in conversation. She discovered that he was an amateur who had taken to stealing because he was out of work. She told him to come back the next morning, and she would see what she could do about getting him a job. When the would-be burglar returned, Addams was able to find him a job.

Finding a job for an unemployed man was just one of the many ways Addams and Starr tried to help their neighbors. They washed newborn babies, nursed the sick, and prepared the dead for burial. They worked to secure financial support for wives deserted by their husbands, insurance for bewildered widows, and damages for injured factory workers. They also took in people in desperate circumstances. For example, a fifteen-year-old bride once sought shelter at Hull House to escape her husband who had beaten her every night for a week.

The constant activity at Hull House was both exhilarating and exhausting. In the midst of all the confusion, there were still meals to be cooked, floors to be mopped, windows

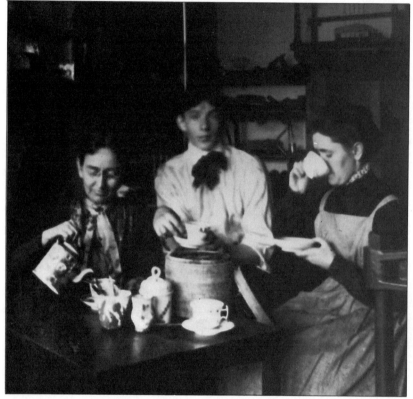

Ellen Starr and Jane Addams in Hull House.

to be washed. Although they had Mary Keyser to help, Addams and Starr performed many of these chores themselves. Little wonder, then, that Addams developed the habit of moving about while she talked, shutting drawers, adjusting pictures, even moving furniture. Gone were the days when she could spend hours curled up by the fire with a book.

When she wasn't talking with Hull House's many visitors, Addams was out giving speeches about the settlement house and the needs of the neighborhood to various groups throughout the city. She worked hard on these speeches, often writing four or five drafts before she was satisfied. She spoke in clear, measured tones. As she delivered her speeches, she would stand with her head slightly forward. She'd either clasp her hands behind her back or finger the necklace she was wearing. More often than not, she looked tired.

As they got to know the neighborhood better, Jane Addams and Ellen Starr were appalled by the terrible conditions under which people lived and worked. For example, in their first six months at Hull House, they met a peasant woman "straight from the fields of Germany." She had spent her four years in the United States carrying pails of water up and down two flights of stairs and washing the heavy flannel suits of foundry workers. For this work, she received thirty-five cents a day.

Addams and Starr learned that the children of such "hard-driven" women as this were either left in the casual care of a neighbor or locked into their tenement rooms. The first three crippled children they met in the neighborhood had all been injured while their mothers were at work. One had fallen out of a third-story window, another had been burned, and a third had a curved spine as a result of having been tied to the leg of a kitchen table each day for three years.

Nevertheless, Addams remained hopeful about the future. She believed that conditions could be improved and also that Chicago was in better shape than most European cities, or even than New York. Addams saw an advantage in the fact that most of the city's large immigrant population were recent arrivals. She noted that Italian and German peasants, who were fresh from their homelands, still put on colorful holiday costumes on Sunday and went out to visit their relatives. They had yet to become downtrodden like the second generation of the city's poor.

Addams soon decided that one goal of the settlement's programs should be to help immigrants preserve the best of their European traditions. She and Starr organized special Italian and German evenings. Families came to sing folk songs, celebrate holidays as they had in their homeland, and share knowledge of their country's history and literature.

Another reason for Jane Addams's optimism in the early months at Hull House was her religious faith. Along with ministers of the Social Gospel movement, Addams believed that the kingdom of God could be advanced on earth by improving conditions and eventually wiping out poverty. She saw Hull House as a religious institution and herself almost as a missionary to the poor.

Since Hull House was located in a largely Roman Catholic neighborhood, no religious services were held there. But Addams often attended the nearby Congregational Church. (She went to this church instead of to a Presbyterian one because it was in the neighborhood, and also because it was struggling.) She also encouraged regular evening Bible and prayer meetings "with everyone on their knees" at Hull House.

Addams had religious faith, but no set theory about what was wrong with society and how it ought to be remedied. She was, however, exposed to a range of such theories.

In the spring of 1890, "The Working People's Social Science Club" began holding regular Wednesday night meetings at Hull House. The club grew out of the large open meetings held after the Haymarket Riot to discuss social problems. It featured a different speaker at each meeting, followed by lively discussions. Speakers included socialists, who believed that the means of producing goods should be publicly owned. Speakers also included anarchists, who called for total freedom for the individual.

Visitors to the club's meetings didn't always realize the differences between views expressed by the speakers and members of the club and those actually held by Jane Addams and other residents of Hull House. Thus, early on, Hull House gained a reputation as a center for radicals—people advocating drastic changes in society.

Jane Addams herself never became a radical. Yet she did come to see that individual and even group acts of kindness were not enough to stem the tide of misery. The change in her outlook came about in part because of the poverty she observed. But most of all, it occurred because of the extraordinary group of people who were drawn to Hull House during its early years.

5

The Hull House Family

As Jane Addams and Ellen Starr had hoped, other young people soon joined them at Hull House. Residents paid their own way. They included men as well as women. Among the men who lived at Hull House at one time or another were Gerard Swope, later president of General Electric; the future historian Charles Beard; and William Lyon Mackenzie King, who later became a prime minister of Canada. But it was the remarkable group of women at Hull House who made the settlement famous and spread its influence far and wide.

Two who came during the first year were Mary Rozet Smith and Julia Lathrop. The daughter of an upper-class Chicago family, Mary Smith was well educated and had been to Europe. But like so many young women of her kind in the late nineteenth century, she felt frustrated by a lack of useful work.

Mary Rozet Smith became Jane Addams's closest friend.

Mary Smith first visited Hull House with her friend, Jenny Dow, the kindergarten teacher. She returned for a lecture and to help out with the kindergarten. Though never an official resident of the settlement, she was soon very much a part of its inner circle.

Mary Smith gave generously of both her time and money. She also became Jane Addams's closest friend, replacing even Ellen Starr in Jane's affections. After the first few years, Jane and Ellen drifted apart. One problem was that Ellen had her own ideas and could be critical of Jane. Mary Smith, on the other hand, was a devoted follower. She was the one Addams turned to when she needed comfort and reassurance. Smith's family became a second family for Addams. Jane was a frequent visitor at the Smith home and sometimes went on trips with Mary's parents.

Like Smith and Addams, Julia Lathrop came from a well-to-do family. Her father was a successful lawyer and politician in Rockford, Illinois. Lathrop's mother was a member of the first graduating class of Rockford Seminary and a supporter of women's suffrage, the right of women to vote. Julia also went to Rockford, but after a year she transferred to Vassar College. Graduating in 1880, she studied in her father's law office, while serving as his secretary and assistant. But living at home and working for her father didn't satisfy Julia. Soon after she learned of Hull House, she moved there.

Julia Lathrop, a small, slight young woman with a somewhat mournful expression, nevertheless, had lots of energy and a sparkling wit. While Addams tended to take herself and her work very seriously, Lathrop could laugh and joke at her own expense. She also demonstrated great organizing ability. At Hull House she helped start a "Plato Club" for the discussion of Greek philosophy with elderly men of the neighborhood. Finally, Lathrop could be counted on in a crisis.

For example, one afternoon, a young woman rushed in to say that a girl in a tenement house down the street was having a baby alone and unassisted. The doctor was late in arriving. None of the women in the neighborhood would help, because the girl was unmarried and considered a disgrace.

Addams and Lathrop anxiously made their way to the tenement. They managed to deliver the baby and quiet the frightened mother. Afterward, Addams protested that they shouldn't have let themselves be rushed into doing something they knew nothing about. Lathrop replied that ignorance should never stand in the way of humanitarian work.

Mary Kenny was a third remarkable woman attracted to Hull House. She belonged to a very different world than did Lathrop, Smith, or Addams herself. Yet Addams befriended the feisty, red-haired young Irish-American woman and from her learned a great deal about the lives of working-class women.

Mary Kenny had to leave school at an early age in order to support her invalid mother. She moved from dressmaking into bookbinding, or the art of fastening pages together, and printing. Kenny helped to organize the first women's bookbinders' union in Chicago. Invited to speak at Hull House, she went reluctantly. But Jane Addams soon won her trust. According to Kenny, Addams was "someone who cared enough to help us and to help us in our way." Addams invited the bookbinders' union to hold their meetings at Hull House. She paid for pamphlets explaining the union and distributed them herself in the shops at noon.

In the spring of 1891, Kenny and Addams decided to start a cooperative boarding club for working girls. When women workers went on strike, they had trouble paying for their room and board. Fearful of being put out on the street, they often backed off in disputes with employers. But as one girl exclaimed at a meeting at Hull House during a strike in a shoe factory, "Wouldn't it be fine if we had a boarding-club of our own, and then we could stand by each other in a time like this?"

Two apartments near Hull House were rented, and fifteen young women moved in. Hull House paid the first month's rent and furnished the apartments. But the "Jane

Club," as it was called, soon became self-supporting. It was one of the first cooperative ventures of its kind to be founded and managed by women.

Another young woman who had a great influence on Jane Addams was Florence Kelley. She came from a background similar to Addams's, but her experience was vastly different. Her father, William D. Kelley, was a Philadelphia judge and congressman. He had earned the nickname "Pig-Iron" because he supported high tariffs—that is, taxes on imported goods. High taxes on foreign-made metal products would make them very expensive. That would help protect the iron and steel industry from foreign competition.

Florence Kelley graduated from Cornell University and went on to the University of Switzerland for advanced study. There she became a socialist. She translated one of the works of the socialist thinker Friedrich Engels into English, married a Polish-Russian doctor, and together with her husband, joined the Socialist Labor party.

After the couple moved to New York, Kelley continued to work for the Socialist party. She lectured and wrote articles in which she attacked the use of young children as factory workers. She had three children of her own, but her marriage was unhappy. In 1891 Kelley left her husband. With her children, she moved to Illinois, where the divorce laws weren't so strict.

Early on a snowy morning between Christmas 1891 and New Year's 1892, Florence Kelley and her children arrived at the door of Hull House. After a few minutes, Addams herself opened the door. In one arm, she held a baby belonging to the cook, who was late with breakfast. With the other arm, she tried to keep an active kindergarten child from dashing out into the snow. Addams welcomed Kelley and her family as warmly as if she had been expecting them all along.

Everyone at Hull House soon felt the demands of Florence Kelley's strong personality. She was a large woman, bursting with energy and burning with indignation—anger at what was unjust. One friend described her as a "smoking volcano." Addams and Lathrop, on the other hand, tended to be soft-spoken and mild-mannered. Yet they often stayed up late at night to listen, talk, and debate with Kelley over cups of hot chocolate. Along with Lathrop, Kelley called Addams "J.A." She respected and admired Addams a great deal. But she was the only one of the group who dared poke fun at Addams or criticize her.

Kelley had little patience with the cultural or the religious side of Hull House. She made fun of the reading parties and evening prayer sessions. Instead, she urged the Hull House group to take an active interest in the reform of working conditions.

While the Hull House family was growing, so was a movement to found other settlement houses. By 1892, six had been started. That summer Jane Addams, Julia Lathrop, and other representatives of the new movement attended a summer school held by the Ethical Culture Society in Plymouth, Massachusetts.

A young man named Robert Woods seemed to be the natural leader of the settlement house group. He was a graduate of Andover Theological Seminary. Woods had returned from a stay in Toynbee Hall to found Andover House (later South End House) in Boston. He had also just written a book on English social movements. Yet despite the impressive backgrounds of Woods and others at the summer school, Addams found herself the center of attention.

Addams made two speeches at the summer school. The first, "The Subjective Necessity for Social Settlements," dealt with the importance of settlement work to the people involved in it. There was in America, Addams said, a growing number of well-educated young people with no worthwhile occupation. Many of them wasted their energies having a good time. Others turned to study simply because they had nothing better to do. In Addams's view, these young people were as deserving of pity as the poor. It was for their benefit as much as that of the poor that settlement houses were needed.

Addams's second address, "The Objective Value of a Social Settlement," described some of the problems she had run into at Hull House, as well as its programs. In between the speeches, there was time for discussion and socializing. Addams and Lathrop spent one beautiful summer afternoon discussing their work with other settlement house residents on the shores of a pond in a pine wood a few miles from Plymouth. The young people were thrilled by the awareness that they now belonged to a national movement.

On the way back to Chicago, Jane Addams stopped in New York City to see if she could find someone to publish her speeches. She was surprised and delighted when the editor of an important magazine in the field agreed right away. The next year her speeches, together with others from the summer school, appeared in book form. The book didn't sell very well. But it helped launch Addams as a writer with a larger audience than she had had before.

Meanwhile, back in Chicago, Florence Kelley was busy uncovering the harsh conditions under which women and young children in the clothing industry worked. The Illinois Bureau of Labor had hired Kelley to make this investigation.

Jane Addams was sometimes called "Lady Jane" by her fellow settlement house workers.

Notebook in hand, she marched into sweatshops—small, dingy factories—where women sat bent over their sewing for as long as twenty hours at a time. In tenement buildings, where families took work home, Kelley found children of four and five spending the entire day pulling out basting threads from the clothes their mothers were sewing. For this labor, the family might receive as little as ten cents an hour. The air in these tenements and sweatshops was hot, stuffy, and foul-smelling. Sometimes a neighbor, family member, or even one of the workers was ill with a highly contagious disease like tuberculois or smallpox.

Kelley's 1892 report on sweatshops led to recommend-ations for the first factory law in Illinois. If passed, this new law would help improve health conditions and cleanliness in sweatshops. Women and children would be allowed to work only eight hours a day, and children under fourteen would not be permitted to work at all in factories.

Addams and the other Hull House residents pushed hard to get this law passed. Every evening for three months during the winter of 1892–93, they addressed open meet-ings of trade unions, benefit societies, and church organiza-tions. While Florence Kelley threw herself into the effort, Addams and Lathrop took part somewhat reluctantly. To get such a law passed required much lobbying—trying to con-vince public officials to vote for the law. Addams found the idea of going before the state legislature to lobby for the proposed law very distasteful. She insisted that several well-known Chicago women accompany the Hull House group to the capitol building.

Factory owners disliked the lobbying efforts of the Hull House residents even more. One wealthy individual even offered to make a contribution of $50,000 to the settlement house—if its members would stop agitating for the factory law. Addams not only refused the bribe but was horrified that she had even been approached. After all, it had been said that her father had been the only man in the Illinois senate who had never been offered a bribe, "because bad men were instinctively afraid of him."

On June 17, 1893, the factory law was passed. Illinois's newly elected reformist governor, John Peter Atgeld, promptly appointed Florence Kelley the chief factory inspector. Her job was to investigate and publicize violations of the new law.

Alzina Stevens, another Hull House resident, served as assistant factory inspector. Like Mary Kenny, Stevens had to go to work at a young age. She learned the printing trade and made a living as a newspaper proofreader and typesetter.

In Chicago, Stevens organized and became the first president of a women's labor group, Working Woman's Union Number 1. She also played an important part in the Knights of Labor, a national labor organization started in 1869. Later, after the Knights went into a decline as a result of the Haymarket Riot, she joined the American Federation of Labor, founded in 1886.

In their work as factory inspectors, Kelley and Stevens exposed many abuses, especially in the area of child labor. They found young boys working as butchers in slaughter houses. The children stood knee-deep in water used to flood the floor, breathing in air that was filled with a sickening stench. They also found many cases of children who had been injured, sometimes fatally, by machinery.

The very year that Kelley and Stevens began their work, a smallpox epidemic broke out in Chicago. Along with Julia

Lathrop, the two women fearlessly entered sweatshops and tenements, where the disease was raging. They did what they could to help the sick and saw that the infected clothing the women and children had been working on was destroyed.

Stevens and Kelley not only lived at Hull House, but Kelley had her office opposite the settlement on Polk Street. Mary Kenny served as one of Kelley's deputy inspectors, and Alexander Bruce, a young lawyer who was a resident at Hull House, prosecuted the cases Kelley brought against violators of the law. Little wonder some Chicagoans considered Hull House "a nest of radicals."

Meanwhile, Julia Lathrop was busy laying bare abuses of another kind. In 1893, Governor Atgeld appointed Lathrop to the Illinois Board of Charities. As a member of this board, Lathrop visited each of the 102 poorhouses in the state. Poorhouses were places where the needy were kept at public expense. She talked with directors, attendants, and inmates and examined records. At one poorhouse, she even slid down the fire-escape chute to test its safety. Lathrop strongly objected to the fact that the young and the old, the sick and the insane were lumped together in the same state institutions. She felt there ought to be separate institutions for delinquent children and hospitals for the insane. She also protested against the employment of attendants without proper training and those appointed for political reasons.

Reformers naturally welcomed the work of Lathrop, Kelley, and other Hull House residents. Henry Demarest Lloyd, a brilliant journalist and muckraker, who exposed social inequality, gave money to the settlement and made speeches there. He introduced Jane Addams to Governor

Atgeld, to the criminal lawyer and reformer Clarence Darrow, and to other labor leaders, politicians, and writers.

Encouragement also came from Richard T. Ely, a professor and well-known writer and lecturer on economic and social problems. Ely was a friend of Florence Kelley's from New York. He urged the Hull House group to conduct systematic investigations of social conditions and publish their findings.

At the time, the idea of studying society in this way was fairly new. Sociology—that is, the study of social institutions and relationships—was a young science. The very term *sociology* had only been coined about fifty years earlier. Still, the Hull House residents had at least one important model to follow in their work. This was Charles Booth's *Labour and Life of the People of London*, one of the first scientific attempts to study a poor section of a major city.

In the summer of 1893, Addams, Kelley, and the other residents began work on a block-by-block, house-by-house survey of the neighborhood around Hull House. They wanted to get information about both the income and the original nationality of the people who lived there. They found that Italians, Russians, Polish Jews, and Germans were the largest immigrant groups in the area. They also discovered that most of their neighbors had a weekly income of from $5 to $10. These findings were indicated by multicolor maps—blue for the Italians, green for the Irish, and so on.

Residents also wrote articles as part of the project. Ellen Starr contributed an essay on "Art and Labor," Julia Lathrop, one on "Cook County Charities," and Addams, an article on "The Settlement as a Factor in the labor Movement." Kelley herself produced the two most blistering articles: "The Sweating System" and, with Alzina Stevens as the other author, "Wage Earning Children."

Some of the residents jokingly referred to the project as "the jumble book." Yet it was a pioneer effort to study a working-class neighborhood in an American city. Published two years later in 1895, *Hull House Maps and Papers* sparked further research on Chicago and other cities.

The project was also important to Addams personally. Although she had only been one of several contributors to *Hull House Maps and Papers*, the work she did helped her see herself as a writer, scholar, and even sociologist.

The summer of 1893 was an especially busy time at Hull House for other reasons as well. Thousands of people from all over the country and abroad flocked to Chicago for the World's Columbian Exposition. This giant fair celebrating the 400th anniversary of Columbus's landing featured six hundred acres of parks, gardens, and stunning, white colonnaded buildings.

When visitors had tired of oohing and aahing over the "Great White City" of the fair, they turned to other "must-see" attractions. These included the Chicago stockyards, where cattle and pigs were kept for slaughter or market, the recently opened University of Chicago, and of course, Hull House.

By this time, Hull House was host to over forty clubs and activities including a day nursery, a playground that was the first in Chicago, an art gallery, a coffee house, and a gymnasium. Every week two thousand people entered its doors.

Among those who visited Hull House that summer were the English socialists Sidney and Beatrice Webb. The Webbs stayed at Hull House and were the guests of honor at a luncheon given by Clarence Darrow. Beatrice Webb was a smoker, and to make her guest feel at home, Jane Addams smoked her first and last cigarette. Mrs. Webb thought Addams "gentle and dignified." But she dismissed the rest of the Hull House group as "all those queer, well-intentioned or cranky individuals."

That summer, too, settlement workers from Boston, Chicago, and New York met in Chicago. Addams acted as chairperson and led the discussions at the various sessions. The meeting further helped to establish her as a leader of the movement. She wrote to a friend that she was considered "the grandmother of social settlements."

Addams and the other early settlement workers saw themselves as pioneers. They were sure their methods were better than those of other charity organizations. They even acted as if they belonged to a religious order, calling each other "Sister Kelley" and "Brother Woods." Addams, though, was "Lady Jane."

The following fall and winter, the resources of Hull House and other settlement houses were tested as never before. At this time, the nation plunged into the worst period of hard times it had yet known. Hundreds of banks were forced to shut their doors, thousands of businesses failed, and millions of people lost their jobs and homes. The depression of 1893 didn't let up until nearly four years later.

Chicago was especially hard hit because of the financial burden of carrying the fair. When the first cold weather came, jobless men who could find no other shelter crowded the police stations and the corridors of the city hall. They held demonstrations to protest their plight by the lakefront.

During this gloomy period, the English journalist and reformer William T. Stead visited Chicago. By day, he roamed the city's bitterly cold streets, filled with unemployed and homeless people. Then late at night, he came to Hull House, tired and hungry. Over a cup of hot chocolate before the fire, he would describe his experiences. For example, one day when he tried to get work as a laborer, he had to stand in line without an overcoat for two hours in the sleet, just for a chance to sweep the streets.

Later Stead wrote a best-selling book, *If Christ Came to Chicago*, based on what he observed that terrible winter of 1893. He concluded that the city's best hope was the spread of settlements like Hull House into all the slum neighborhoods.

While still in Chicago, Stead called a huge meeting of labor leaders, clergy, charity workers, and city officials. The result was a temporary organization that later developed into the Civic Federation of Chicago.

Jane Addams was a member of the committee of five appointed to carry out the suggestions made at the meeting. The committee set up employment stations to provide the jobless with work—sewing for the women and street sweeping for the men. It also found temporary lodging for those with no place to stay. Hull House itself gave shelter to homeless women whom no one else would take in. Finally, the committee established relief stations at Hull House and other locations. Here the desperately needy came for money to keep their families from starving.

For Addams, one of the most painful episodes of the winter involved an unemployed shipping clerk who had come to Hull House several times for relief. One day when the man appeared, Addams told him about a job digging a drainage canal. He replied that he had always worked indoors and didn't think he could take the exposure of an outdoor job. Addams explained that she wasn't supposed to give out relief to anyone who could find work. The man took the canal-digging job, but after two days, he caught pneumonia and died.

Hard as times were that winter, worse was yet to come. In the early months of the depression, different groups had at least cooperated to relieve the misery. But before long, this cooperation vanished, as a violent upheaval ripped the city apart. Addams and the Hull House residents found themselves on one side. Many of their supporters among the wealthy and prominent were on the other.

In the summer of 1894, a bitter labor dispute broke out at the Pullman Palace Car Company near Chicago. The company manufactured sleeping and dining cars for railroads. Its owner, George M. Pullman, was considered a model employer. He had built a company town for his workers. It had pleasant housing, a library, lakes, parks, and gardens. But when the depression hit, Pullman cut wages by as much as 40 percent. He didn't, however, lower the high rents workers had to pay at the company town. With rents eating up their wages, workers had practically no money left over for food and clothing. They appealed to Pullman to either lower rents or raise wages, but he refused.

In June, the Pullman workers went on strike. Eugene V. Debs, a tall, fiery young railroad worker, supported them. The year before, Debs had organized the American Railway Union, which soon had a membership of 150,000. Debs told the members of his union to disconnect all Pullman cars from the trains on which they worked. The railroads fought back by firing any railway employee who did so. But when an employee was fired, the whole train crew quit in protest. Before long, the entire national rail system had ground to an almost complete halt.

In Chicago and elsewhere, feelings ran high against the striking workers. For example, when Jane Addams was coming down in an elevator one day, she met an acquaintance who angrily declared "that all strikers ought to be shot." With violence threatening, various individuals and groups tried desperately to settle the dispute. The newly created Civic Federation of Chicago appointed an investigating committee. Addams was on this committee. She went to the town of Pullman on her own, because its managers refused to see the whole committee. She found that the workers did, indeed, have cause to complain. Yet when she suggested that an impartial board be appointed to investigate the workers' grievances, she was told to mind her own business.

In July, a family crisis forced Addams to do just that. She received word that her oldest sister, Mary, who was recovering from a long illness in a hospital in Kenosha, Wisconsin, had taken a turn for the worse. Addams was able to reach her sister at once, but Mary's husband and children, who lived farther away, were delayed by the railroad strike. Addams comforted her sister and took care of most of her hospital expenses. After her sister's death, she devoted a large portion of her income to Mary's four children. Still, her sister Alice often complained that she wasn't doing enough.

Meanwhile, the strike turned violent. The railroad owners brought in strikebreakers. They also got U.S. Attorney General Richard Olney to appoint 3,400 special deputies to keep the trains running. Strikers clashed with the strikebreakers and federal deputies, blocking trains and burning railway cars.

While Eugene Debs tried to stop the violence, Governor Atgeld fought to keep the U.S. Army from intervening. But President Grover Cleveland sent in troops to restore order and see that the U.S. mail was delivered. When Addams returned to the city, one of the first things she saw were these blue-coated soldiers camped out near the post office. But when she arrived at Halstead Street, she saw just about everyone wearing a white ribbon to show their support of the strikers. The presence of the troops led to more violence, however. A federal judge then ordered an end to the strike. Debs was thrown into jail for refusing to obey this order. The strike collapsed.

When Debs was temporarily released from jail, Florence Kelley and Alzina Stevens protected him from the public and the press. Kelley also tried to organize a mass meeting to raise money for his legal defense. But most people thought Debs a dangerous radical and wouldn't have anything to do with him.

For her part, Addams wanted very much to understand how such a terrible tragedy as the Pullman strike could have occurred. She made a speech about the strike at the Chicago Women's Club and other organizations. The title of her speech was "A Modern Lear." In it, she compared George Pullman to King Lear, the main character in one of Shakespeare's tragedies. King Lear had given up his wealth to his daughters. Just as Lear viewed himself as a generous parent toward his daughters, so Pullman saw himself in regard to his employees. Like Lear, Pullman had an exaggerated notion of his own kindness that blinded him to the real needs of his workers. When they tried to explain these needs to him, he angrily accused them of being ungrateful.

But if Pullman was in the wrong, so was the labor

movement, Addams said. Both sides needed to learn to work together. Overall, Addams's message was a mild one. Yet the violence of the strike had turned public opinion so strongly against the railway workers that no one would publish her speech. Addams's stand also lost her the financial support of George Pullman and other wealthy backers of Hull House.

In the Pullman and later strikes, Addams always tried to find the reasonable middle ground. She disliked strikes and violence. Instead, she favored the peaceful settlement of disputes, along with laws to improve the workers' lot. Jane Addams's sympathy with workers never led her to join the picket lines as frail, artistic Ellen Starr did. This simply wasn't her way of doing things.

CHAPTER

6

A Practical Reformer

Jane Addams's ability to see both sides of a question sometimes disappointed and annoyed friends and co-workers. They wanted her to take more of a definite stand. Ellen Starr once described Jane Addams this way: "Jane if the devil himself came riding down Halstead Street with his tail waving out behind him, you'd say 'what a beautiful curve he has in his tail.'"

Starr exaggerated, of course. Addams was deeply concerned about social problems and determined to do something about them. Among the problems that concerned her in the early years of Hull House was the huge amount of garbage in the neighborhood. Slaughterhouses, bakeries, fruit and vegetable vendors, and residents all dumped their refuse into the streets. City collectors were supposed to remove the garbage. But they didn't come around on a regular basis. So the wooden collection boxes were soon

The poorest children spent hours searching the Chicago dumps for food to eat.

filled with a stinking mess of filth. Neighborhood children played their games in and around these boxes. The situation was so bad that Addams was afraid to have her youngest nephew, of whom she was now the legal guardian, come and stay with her at Hull House.

What was to be done? Addams and the other residents had already set up an incinerator at Hull House. They had also given many talks to their immigrant neighbors about the importance of proper waste disposal. But these efforts hadn't done much good.

In the summer of 1894, the Hull House residents

decided to conduct an investigation of the city's system of garbage collection. They found 1,037 violations of sanitary laws in the ward and reported these to the health department. As a result, three city inspectors were transferred from the Nineteenth Ward for failure to do their jobs properly. Nevertheless, the problem persisted.

The following spring, "in sheer desperation," Addams put in a bid for the removal of garbage in the nineteenth ward. Her bid was thrown out on a technicality. But the resulting publicity made the mayor decide to appoint Addams ward garbage inspector at a salary of $1,000 a year. For this—the only paid position she ever held—Addams rose at six every morning. In a horse and buggy, she followed the angry collector on his rounds, making sure he emptied every one of the wooden garbage boxes.

Addams held this post for less than a year. (She ended up hiring for the next three years a deputy to whom she paid over her entire salary.) Yet in Addams's six years at Hull House, nothing so captured the public's imagination as her work as a garbage inspector. More than anything else, it established her reputation as a practical reformer.

Still, the streets didn't get a lot cleaner. Nor did the Nineteenth Ward's death rate—one of the highest in the city—drop very much. Addams herself was stricken with typhoid fever in the fall of 1895.

Her recovery was slow. To hasten it, she decided to take a trip to Europe with Mary Smith in the summer of 1896. The two women went first to England, where they visited with leaders of various social movements. Then they traveled to Russia so Addams could meet a man she had long admired. Count Leo Tolstoy was a famous Russian author, philosopher, and reformer. He fascinated Addams because, though of noble birth and accustomed to luxury, he had chosen to live the very hard life of a Russian peasant.

Unfortunately, Addams's visit to Tolstoy's country estate didn't go very well. She and Tolstoy had barely been introduced when he grabbed at the sleeve of her dress. He said there was enough material in that one sleeve to make an entire dress for a little girl. Didn't she find such a dress "a barrier to the people"? he demanded. Much embarrassed, Addams tried to explain that huge as her sleeves were, those worn by most working girls in Chicago were even bigger. Thus nothing would separate her more from "the people" than if she wore a plain cotton blouse. Besides, even if she had wanted to dress as a peasant, she would have trouble choosing her style of peasant clothing from among the thirty-six different nationalities who lived in the nineteenth ward.

Tolstoy, however, was relentless. Next, he wanted to know how she got her food and shelter. Addams replied that the money she lived on came from a farm a hundred miles from Chicago. So she was an absentee landlord, Tolstoy cried. Didn't she think she could help people more by farming her own land instead of adding herself to the crowded city? Addams felt even more uncomfortable when Tolstoy's daughter returned from the fields, where she had been working with a group of peasants since five in the morning.

Addams wasn't convinced everyone ought to live like Tolstoy. But while still on her trip, she made plans to spend at least two hours every morning baking bread in the Hull House bakery. She had learned this skill as a child. Her miller-father had insisted that each of his daughters present him with a homemade loaf of bread on her twelfth birthday. Yet once back in Chicago, Addams gave up her plans for "bread labor" as "utterly preposterous." She simply had too many other important things to do.

For example, there was Johnny Powers, the corrupt political boss of the Nineteenth Ward, to be reckoned with. A short, stocky Irish American with a gray pompadour, "De Pow," as he was called, had enormous influence. He was chairman of the finance committee of the Chicago city council and head of the Cook County Democratic party. He was also an unashamed "boodler"—that is, he was ever ready to accept a bribe in exchange for his influence or vote. Thus on a salary of three dollars a week, Powers was able to own two large saloons, a gambling establishment, a fine house, and a flashy collection of diamonds.

Johnny Powers was about as dishonest as a city official could be. But to the immigrant residents of the Nineteenth Ward, he was, first and foremost, a friend. At Christmastime, Powers gave out free turkeys. When there was a death in a family, he paid for the funeral. He found jobs for people who were out of work. He put up bail money for those who had been arrested and sent to jail. These actions won him the unquestioning loyalty of the neighborhood and made him a difficult man to challenge.

But challenge Powers the Hull House residents did. In 1895, a Hull House resident had run for a seat on the city legislature on a reform ticket. Although he won the election, he let Powers bribe him and become another of the boss's supporters.

In 1896, however, the Hull House residents launched a campaign to unseat Powers himself. They put forward their own candidate, an Irish-American member of the Hull

House Men's Club. They also plastered the neighborhood with posters and placards denouncing Powers as "the prince of boodlers." The Hull House candidate lost. But residents were cheered by the fact that Powers had won by a smaller number of votes than he had in the past.

Two years later, Addams fired the opening shots in another campaign against Powers. She made a speech before the Ethical Culture Society, in which she not only attacked Powers, but offered a shrewd analysis of his appeal to voters. Removing Powers from office wouldn't be easy, Addams concluded. It would take a change in the moral standards of the community. It would also require a new understanding on the part of reformers. They had to be ready to develop the kind of personal relationships with voters that were the key to Powers's success.

This time Powers counterattacked. He claimed that Addams was jealous of his charitable work in the ward. He also predicted that Hull House would be driven from the ward, and its leaders forced "to shut up shop." Joining Powers in the attack on Hull House were a local newspaper, the *Chicago Chronicle*, and some of the Roman Catholic priests in the neighborhood. They charged that Hull House was anti-Catholic and anti-immigrant. Posters and placards denounced "petticoat government." Addams personally received plenty of "hate mail."

In the election, Addams supported a reform candidate who was a Catholic Irish American and a member of the Democratic party. He had lived in the ward for thirty years. Even so, Powers won by a larger margin than in 1896. Crowed the reelected boss: "I may not be the sort of man that reformers like, but I am what my people like, and neither Hull House nor all the reformers in town can turn them against me."

Having failed twice to unseat Powers, Addams decided to cut her losses. She had learned important lessons about the limits of reform in her ward. Now she wanted to share these lessons with the rest of the world.

The next few years were some of the busiest of Addams's life. She crisscrossed the country, making many speeches and improving her platform skills. On these speaking tours, she was usually accompanied by Mary Smith, Florence Kelley, or Louise de Koven Bowen. Bowen was a wealthy Chicago matron who had been involved with Hull House since 1893.

Addams needed the companionship of these women, but her privacy was also important to her. Louise Bowen discovered this on a trip she took with Addams and another woman. At one crowded hotel, the three women had to share one room, which had a closet and a bath. Addams went into the unlighted closet to undress, took a bath, and went to bed. Her two companions followed suit. The next morning, the same procedure was repeated. Addams got up, shut herself in the closet, and came out fully dressed with her hair neatly arranged. Louise Bowen wondered if she would have to do this every time she traveled with a social worker.

Despite her hectic schedule, Addams continued to manage Hull House, supervising the almost constant remodeling and starting new programs. By 1899—Hull House's tenth anniversary—the original building had been completely remodeled and a third floor added. New buildings included the Children's Building, for which Mary Smith gave the money, a building for the Jane Club, made possible by another wealthy donor, a new coffeehouse, and over it, the Hull House Theater.

With so many buildings and programs, the settlement was in constant need of money. Addams wrote hundreds of letters requesting contributions and then thanking people for them. Her friends joked that they never received more than a one-page letter from her. The reason was that she wrote so many one-page letters in connection with contributions.

Without Addams's considerable skills as a fund-raiser and administrator, Hull House would not have lasted long. Her upper-class background helped in getting money from wealthy Chicagoans. But she also showed extraordinary tact and patience in her dealings with donors. For example, through careful diplomacy, Addams was able to get Helen Culver, the owner of Hull House, to make needed repairs. Addams even convinced her to allow them the use of Hull House rent free. When that rent agreement ended, Culver continued to extend the rent-free lease. Eventually, Culver gave all of the nearby property to Hull House.

One person Addams wasn't able to talk into contributing to the settlement was her stepmother. Anna Addams steadfastly refused to give any money to Hull House. And Jane herself only made matters worse when she suggested that if her father had lived, *he* would have done so.

In 1901, however, Addams took a stand that cost her the support of a number of long-time donors. That year, President William McKinley was assassinated by Leon Czolgosz, who admitted to being an anarchist. The president's murder produced a wave of hysteria. It was particularly strong in Chicago, where the memory of Haymarket Riot was still fresh. Police rounded up and arrested hundreds of people, mostly immigrants suspected of holding radical views.

Among them was Abraham Isaaks, a Russian immigrant and leader of a society of philosophical anarchists. Issaks was a quiet, scholarly man in his mid-fifties who had a wife and family. He edited a paper called *Free Society* and often attended lectures and discussions at Hull House and another settlement, the Chicago Commons.

On the night McKinley was shot, police entered Isaaks's apartment, arresting him and his family. They destroyed his printing presses and confiscated his books, including his volumes of Shakespeare, on the grounds that they were radical literature. The first to learn of Isaaks's arrest was Raymond Robbins, a young settlement worker at Chicago Commons. He appealed to Jane Addams, and together they tried to get Issaks freed on bail. When this failed, they went directly to Mayor Carter Harrison, Jr. The mayor insisted that it wasn't safe to let Isaaks see a lawyer, but he did allow Addams to visit the editor in jail. She did her best to reassure him and was finally able to get him a lawyer. As a result, the Isaaks family was soon released from prison.

Addams's role in the affair brought her a great deal of negative publicity. One newspaper declared that her support of the anarchist "firebrand" showed a lack of judgment and would lessen Addams's influence in humanitarian work. Others expressed their anger by throwing stones through the windows of Hull House and Chicago Commons. Among those who withdrew their support from Hull House at this time was the "queen" of Chicago society, Bertha Honoré Palmer.

Such criticism didn't stop Addams from taking up the

case of another so-called anarchist several years later. Aver-buch, a nineteen-year-old Russian Jewish immigrant, was shot and killed by the chief of police when he went to the chief's house, alone and unarmed. The chief declared that Averbuch had come to assassinate him and that he had fired in self-defense. In the panic that followed, Averbuch's sister Olga was arrested, printing offices in the Russian Jewish community ransacked, and tenements searched.

Jane Addams turned to a young lawyer recommended by a friend for help. The lawyer was Harold Ickes (who later became the secretary of the interior under President Frank-lin Roosevelt). Ickes saw that legal justice was done, while Addams calmed the terrified members of the Russian Jewish community. She also made speeches and wrote an article defending the right of the settlements to allow anarchists and other radicals to speak.

Jane Addams's defense of anarchists and other so-called radicals made her unpopular in Chicago. Nationally, how-ever, her reputation as a reformer was growing steadily. In the first ten years at Hull House, she had made a name for herself chiefly as a speaker. In the next ten years, she did so as a writer.

In 1902, Addams published her first book, *Democracy and Social Ethics*. The book was based on lectures she had given, most of them first published as articles in such magazines as the *Atlantic Monthly* and the *American Journal of Sociology*.

In this book, Addams put forward a broader interpreta-tion of democracy that went beyond the right to vote. She was concerned with relationships among people. Every person, Addams argued, whatever his or her background or occupation, deserved to be treated as the equal of all others.

Thus the person who gave out charity shouldn't act superior to the poor person who received it. People were poor, Addams wrote, not because they were vicious and lazy, but because of social conditions and the effect of their environment on them.

Addams also made the case for more democratic relationships between employers and their employees, between parents and their children—especially their unmarried daughters—and between the political reformers and ordinary citizens. If all these people could accept democracy and uphold the common humanity of their fellows, this would be reform enough, Addams concluded.

The book was enthusiastically received. The American philosopher and psychologist William James hailed it as "one of the great books of our time." "You utter instinctively the truth we others vainly seek," he told Addams.

Two years later in 1904, William James and Jane Addams shared the platform at an important peace conference in Boston. Addams's concern with peace went back to the Spanish-American War of 1898. That war, which was supposedly fought to free Cuba from Spain's corrupt rule, ended with the United States in control of Cuba and other Spanish colonies like the Philippines. The evils of the war were apparent to Addams in the neighborhood of Hull House, where an increase in murders occurred and where she saw children "playing war."

Addams hoped to find a substitute for the warlike spirit in human nature or, as William James put it, "the moral equivalent for war." She decided to write a book on the subject. The writing went slowly, in part because Addams had trouble developing and stating her ideas and in part because she was busy with so many other things. But in 1905, she and Mary Smith purchased a cottage near Bar Harbor, Maine, and spent the first of many summers there. In this remote, rural setting, Addams found the peace and quiet she needed to put her thoughts into writing.

Newer Ideals of Peace came out in 1907. Addams began by attacking the "older dovelike ideal" of peace as too passive and ineffective. Instead, she wanted to put forward "more aggressive ideals of peace." Addams found hope in the coming of a new industrial age. In this new age, she believed, the peaceful instincts and cooperative spirit of working men and women would prevent war. She also argued that giving women the vote would serve this purpose. Women's motherly feelings made them naturally opposed to war, Addams declared.

Not surprisingly, William James praised the book. Others, however, greeted it with indifference or outright criticism. One was President Theodore Roosevelt. He called Addams "Foolish Jane Addams" and attacked the book in an essay, though without mentioning it by name. Roosevelt's reaction was to be expected. In the Spanish-American War, he had raised and led a special cavalry unit known as the Rough Riders.

Addams's third book, *The Spirit of Youth and City Streets*, was a much bigger success. It was also the one she claimed was her favorite. Published in 1909, the book reflected Addams's long-standing concern with the problems of young people living in cities.

This concern had led Addams and the other Hull House residents to set up a variety of programs. They had started a playground and offered all kinds of clubs, classes, and recreational activities. Nevertheless, young people in the neighborhood often got into trouble with the law. Addams and the other settlement workers were bothered by the fact that youthful offenders were often arrested for minor offenses and then thrown into jail with hardened criminals. They decided that something needed to be done to change this system.

The Hull House residents had pushed for a new law, which in 1899 set up the first juvenile court in the country. This court wasn't a criminal court. Rather it was supposed to keep the rights and interests of young offenders firmly in mind. The judge could put the delinquent on probation—that is, let him or her go free on good behavior. He could also put the delinquent under the protection of the state or assign him or her to an institution. The idea was to help rather than punish juvenile offenders. Alzina Stevens of Hull House served as the first probation officer of the court. At first Julia Lathrop, then Louise Bowen, chaired the juvenile court committee.

The Spirit of Youth and City Streets drew upon material collected by the juvenile court, as well as upon Addams's own observations of Chicago youth and her memories of her own childhood and youth. She felt that the city offered many temptations to young people. There were brightly colored theater posters, loud street music, trashy love stories, and such things as revolvers displayed in pawnshop windows. Too often, Addams wrote, these temptations led young people to a life of crime. She believed there ought to be more socially acceptable outlets for the natural impulses of youth. For example, recreation centers and settlement houses could provide an alternative to the saloons; parks, playgrounds, and team sports, to the thrills supplied by liquor and drugs.

Addams also blamed the industrial system, under which young people worked all day long at boring tasks. Factories, she realized, were there to stay. But she wanted working conditions improved so that machines didn't destroy the people who ran them. Addams also favored a team spirit. A number of people working on the same product could appreciate how their particular task contributed to the whole.

The book's positive message made it very popular. Again the greatest tribute came from William James. "The fact is, Madam," he wrote Addams, "that you are not like the rest of us, who seek the truth and try to express it. You *inhabit* reality." The year the book came out, Addams received a further honor when she was appointed the first woman president of the National Conference of Charities and Corrections.

Looking back on this period of her life, Addams was proud of everything she had accomplished—except for her four years on the Chicago school board. The mayor had appointed Addams to the board in 1905, because of her reputation as a reformer. She became chairperson of the school management committee. This committee was responsible for teacher promotion, curriculum, supplies, and salaries. Right away, Addams got into trouble.

The difficulty arose over the issue of teacher promotion. Under the system then in use, the only way teachers could advance was to take a special exam. However, they weren't allowed to take that exam unless they had received a high rating from the principal. The teachers' federation wanted a fairer system that would remove teacher evaluation from politics. Their plan did away with the exam and substituted observations by the teacher's superintendent, another superintendent, and a third party.

At first, Addams appeared to approve this new plan.

But when it aroused much controversy, she ended up voting for a compromise proposal. The head of the teachers' federation was furious. So were others who felt that Addams had failed to stand for principle.

Two years later, Addams again ran into trouble with the reform members of the board. A new mayor had taken office, and one of his first actions was to fire almost all the reform members of the school board except Addams. The fired members expected Addams to spring to their defense and resign in protest. When she didn't, they were enraged.

Addams's willingness to compromise might ruffle feathers locally, but on the national level, she was regarded as a great moral leader. In 1909, Hull House celebrated its twentieth birthday. Therefore, it seemed fitting that Addams should reflect on the experiences of those years in print. She did so in a book published the following year, when she was fifty years old.

The year got off to a bad start, because in December 1909, Addams was hospitalized with an attack of appendicitis. Her recovery was slow and painful. For two months she couldn't work. Fortunately, though, she had already completed much of the writing on her autobiography, *Twenty Years at Hull House*. As early as 1905, Addams had begun working on it. A year later, she published three articles, containing most of the highlights, in *Ladies Home Journal*.

The response to these articles was overwhelmingly favorable. Hundreds of women wrote Addams to tell her how much they admired her. Other magazines picked up the story, one going so far as to proclaim her "The Only Saint America Has Produced."

The notion of Addams as a saint wasn't new. As early as

1893, a few people had begun calling Addams "Saint Jane." And women of the Hull House neighborhood—especially Italian Americans whose Roman Catholic religion included the honoring of saints—often treated Addams in a very special way. She was called on to preside at funerals and weddings, and sometimes even filled in for Protestant ministers in the pulpit on Sundays.

The emphasis on Addams's saintliness annoyed some of those around her. "Do you know what I would do if that woman calls you a saint again?" cried an exasperated Florence Kelley on one occasion. "I'd show her my teeth, and if that didn't convince her, I would bite her."

Yet far from annoying or embarrassing Addams, this lavish praise and adoration gave her confidence and a sense that what she was doing was important. Indeed, she seemed to need it to go forward. She carefully saved the letters and newspaper articles that glorified her the most. These she put in envelopes marked "Articles about J.A." She also kept a scrapbook about Hull House and her own activities. One of the residents had the job of keeping this scrapbook up to date. In addition, Addams subscribed to a clipping service so as not to miss any magazine articles or newspaper accounts of her achievements. When the number of clippings began to get out of hand, she enlisted her sister Alice's help in organizing them.

Addams used the information in her scrapbook and clipping files as well as her own recollections in writing her autobiography. The first part of the book told the personal story of how she came to found Hull House. The second part described the activities of the settlement house. There were many tales of poor and unhappy people. Yet the overall message of the book was optimistic. Addams was convinced that American democracy would not only survive the challenges that came with the growth of cities and massive immigration from abroad, but grow stronger as a result. To the thousands who read *Twenty Years at Hull House*, Addams herself seemed to stand for the success of American democracy.

On a golden October afternoon that same year of 1910, Addams took a seat on the platform at Smith College alongside a much older celebrity. Ninety-five-year-old reformer Julia Ward Howe had written the famous song "Battle Hymn of the Republic" in the early 1860s when Jane Addams was not even two years old. Now Smith College wanted to honor these two champions of American democracy by awarding them special degrees. When Howe's turn came, the organ pealed and a chorus of some two thousand girls in white dresses broke out with "Mine eyes have seen the glory of the coming of the Lord...."

7

"Enlisted for the Great Battle"

The year 1912 was a particularly busy one for Jane Addams. In the spring, she published yet another book. In the summer and fall, she took part in her first national political campaign.

Addams's new book was called *A New Conscience and an Ancient Evil.* In it, she tackled the controversial subject of prostitution—that is, the practice of engaging in sexual relations for money. Many of Addams's friends didn't like the idea of her writing about such a troubling topic. But Addams was convinced she had something important to say. While she was no expert on the subject, her years at Hull House had certainly made her aware of the problem. Also, she had read many of the case studies collected by the juvenile protection association. Among its goal was the control or outright closing of such supposed breeders of vice and crime as poolrooms, bars, and dance halls.

Jane Addams presented her controversial ideas to a vast public by means of lectures, magazine articles, and books.

In her book, Addams presented prostitution as an ancient evil made worse by the conditions of an urban, industrial society. However, she praised the growth of a reform movement, or "new conscience," that would do away with this evil. Addams was convinced that no woman became a prostitute voluntarily. Rather, she viewed prostitutes as the innocent victims of economic circumstances.

For example, in her book Addams told the story of an "honest, straightforward" girl who had come to Chicago from a small town in northern Michigan. The girl worked in a café in the city and sent half her wages home to help her mother and her little sister who had tuberculosis. Learning from her mother that her sister was near death, the girl wanted to get home and see her sister one last time. However, she didn't have enough money for the trip. In the end, she agreed to accompany a local businessman on the night boat, if he would pay her return fare. The girl reached home before her sister's death, but returned to Chicago, burdened with the debt of the undertaker's bill. Recalling her experience with the businessman on the night boat, she realized she had discovered a means of paying this and other bills.

Addams maintained that if women like this poor girl were paid adequate salaries, they wouldn't be forced into prostitution. Moreover, if women were given the vote, they wouldn't tolerate this ancient evil.

A few people were shocked by Addams's book. But most responded favorably. They felt that Addams had treated a difficult subject with great tact and delicacy.

Addams wasn't alone in arguing that if women had the vote prostitution and other social and economic evils would end. An organized women's suffrage movement had existed in the United States since right after the Civil War. Rockford College, when Addams went there, had been a center of suffrage sentiment. Yet Addams didn't join the National American Woman Suffrage Association (NAWSA) until 1906.

Since that time, Addams had made many speeches on behalf of women's getting the vote. She had campaigned unsuccessfully for city women's suffrage in Chicago and also for woman suffrage in all elections in Illinois. Together with over three hundred other women, she had boarded a train and traveled to the state capital at Springfield to argue the case for woman suffrage before the legislature. In 1911, she had been elected a vice president of the NAWSA. Now in 1912, she spoke at the organization's annual convention in Philadelphia.

That year, 1912, was an election year. So Addams and other suffragists hoped to get the Republicans to support woman suffrage in the platform they drew up at their national convention.

Another reform-minded organization that wanted to get the Republicans to back its program was the National Conference of Charities and Correction. In 1909, the same year that Addams had been elected its president, this organization had appointed a committee on standards in the workplace. Florence Kelley, who had moved to New York and was now a resident at Lillian Wald's Henry Street Settlement House, was a member of this committee. The committee began a three-year study of conditions in industry.

Meanwhile, a Hull House resident, Dr. Alice Hamilton, had been conducting her own investigation of diseases that affected workers in various industries. She discovered that

Jane Addams took part in parades and other activities, demanding that women have the right to vote.

workers whose jobs involved contact with lead products became very ill and were, in effect, poisoned by this contact. She and her assistants identified 77 industrial processes that used lead and 578 victims of lead poisoning. As a result of her investigations, the state of Illinois passed a law protecting workers in the so-called poisonous trades in 1911.

The following year, the committee on standards in industry brought out its report. The work of Dr. Hamilton and others had convinced the committee of the need for better health and safety measures in factories. Because some workers, especially women and children, were paid less than six dollars a week, the committee also called for a minimum wage. It demanded an eight-hour workday and a six-day workweek. (This was at a time when small children in some cotton mills worked as long as sixty-six hours a week.) Children under sixteen were not to be allowed to work in factories at all. Finally, there was to be a federal program of financial support for the unemployed, as well as for workers who had to leave their jobs because of injury or old age.

In June 1912, the Republicans held their national convention in Chicago. A group of social workers presented their program of industrial standards to the party's platform committee. But the committee wasn't interested. Jane Addams did little better when she went before the platform committee in behalf of women's suffrage. The committee telephoned her just an hour before she was supposed to appear. Arriving breathlessly with a group of other local suffrage leaders, she was told she could have five minutes and present one speaker. The Republican platform ended up not supporting women's suffrage.

But if the Republicans refused to back either women's suffrage or industrial reforms, a new party did. It was called the Progressive party. In 1912, this party was launched by reformers within the Republican party who were unhappy with the Republicans' choice of a candidate. As its candidate, the Progressive party chose former President Theodore Roosevelt. The party also became known as the Bull Moose party after Roosevelt declared that he felt "strong as a bull moose."

Jane Addams had met Roosevelt on several previous occasions. The exuberant former president had twice visited Hull House. The first time he had come to review a huge assembly of Boy Scouts at Hull House's largest hall. After the review, Addams and Roosevelt went over to the armory to address a meeting of immigrants. At the crowded meeting, Addams lost her hat. To make her feel more comfortable as they rode back in an open motor car, Roosevelt went hatless, too. The newspapers picked up the story and had a field day with it. One paper joked that Addams's carelessness with hats was one of the reasons she hadn't been able to get a husband.

In 1909, Addams had been invited to Washington to attend a special conference on the care of dependent children called by then President Roosevelt. As the evening speakers were waiting to go up onto the platform, the young man in charge became flustered. "Are we all here?" he asked. "Yes, here is my Catholic speaker, my Jewish speaker, the Protestant, the colored man, and the woman." At this, Addams turned to the African-American leader, Booker T. Washington, and said, "You see, I am last; that is because I have no vote." Replied Washington: "I am glad to know the reason. I have always before been the end of such a procession myself."

According to Addams, Roosevelt had a good chuckle over the incident. She may not have found it so amusing herself. But she was pleased by Roosevelt's efforts in the area of social justice. For example, as president, Roosevelt had brought the power of the federal government to bear not on the striking workers but on the mine owners during the coal strike of 1902. When the mine owners refused to deal with the miners' union, Roosevelt threatened to send the army in. The mine owners gave in, and the miners went back to work and later won most of their demands.

As the leader of the Progressive party, Roosevelt now promised to support both a program of industrial reforms and women's suffrage. Little wonder then that Addams and many other reformers eagerly joined the party's ranks.

The Progressive party held its national convention in Chicago in August 1912. The convention turned out to be one of the most exciting in American history. Enthusiastic delegates waved flags and banners and sang "Roosevelt Oh Roosevelt" to the tune of "Maryland My Maryland," and hymns like "Onward Christian Soldiers." Indeed, the atmosphere was more like that of a religious revival meeting than a political convention. For Addams and other reformers, the convention seemed to mark the highest point of years of struggle to obtain social justice.

Nevertheless, the convention had its difficult moments for Addams. As a delegate and member of the platform committee, she was forced to accept two measures that went against her concern for world peace. One measure, or plank, called for building two battleships a year. The other, which Addams found even more difficult to "swallow," called for fortifying the Panama Canal. The U.S. government had worked very hard to secure the health and lives of the workers who had dug the canal, Addams said. Now it shouldn't build on the same spot huge fortifications that threatened people with destruction. But both planks passed and became part of the party's platform.

Addams was also upset when Roosevelt decided that blacks couldn't be active members of the party in the South. She had long sympathized with the problems faced by African Americans. Few African Americans lived in the Hull House neighborhood. But when the National Association of Colored Women met in Chicago in 1899, Addams had invited them to lunch at Hull House. Booker T. Washington, the black leader and founder of the Tuskegee Institute, had also been a guest at Hull House. Finally, Addams was close friends with two of the founders of the National Association for the Advancement of Colored People (NAACP). Although she wasn't present at the first meeting of this organization in 1909, she was made a member of its executive committee. The NAACP worked through the courts to end restrictions on voting and other injustices suffered by African Americans.

At the Progressive party convention, Addams helped draft a plank on the rights of African Americans and fought to get it adopted. The platform committee debated the plank throughout an all-night session. But in the end, the plank was defeated. Later, Roosevelt himself recalled that Addams came very close to leaving the party over this issue.

Addams not only stayed, but was persuaded to second Roosevelt's nomination. When she rose to make her speech in the packed Chicago coliseum, she was greeted almost as enthusiastically as the candidate himself. Delegates clapped, cheered, and stamped their feet.

Dressed simply in white, Addams spoke quietly and calmly. Most of her speech was devoted to praising the platform. "A great party," Addams said, "has pledged itself to the protection of children, to the care of the aged, to the relief of overworked girls, to the safeguarding of burdened men." Given these noble goals, she continued, it was inevitable that the party would appeal to women and seek to draw on their moral energy. Addams didn't mention Roosevelt until the end of her speech. And then her words were carefully chosen. She told her listeners that she seconded Roosevelt's nomination because he was one of the few men in public life who supported the movement for social justice.

When Addams stepped down from the platform, the auditorium rang with cheers—more for Addams herself than for Roosevelt. A group of women handed her a large yellow banner that read Votes for Women, and as she made her way to her seat, women stepped in behind her. While the procession marched down the aisle, other women in the audience waved their handkerchiefs and cried out their approval. This spontaneous demonstration lasted for several minutes.

Although others made nominating speeches for Roosevelt, Addams's speech received the most attention in the press. It wasn't so much what she said as what she represented. One newspaper printed a cartoon showing Roosevelt and Addams shaking hands, surrounded by figures labeled "poverty," "old age," and "child labor." The caption read: "Enlisted for the Great Battle."

Having helped launch this "great battle," Jane Addams threw herself into it with vigor. She wrote a number of articles about the Progressive party and its platform. And that September, she joined the campaign. Addams made speeches in New York and Boston, then conducted a whirlwind tour of the major cities of the Midwest. She even spoke in places like Leadville, Colorado, and Fargo, North Dakota, and in small towns throughout Iowa, Nebraska, and Missouri.

Some newspapers estimated Addams's value to Roosevelt at a million votes. Addams, however, said this was a great exaggeration. Yet everywhere she went, large and enthusiastic crowds greeted her. In Los Angeles, California, a group of women even organized a "Jane Addams Chorus" to sing at Progressive rallies. Women in other cities did the same. The choruses featured hundreds of women dressed all in white, who sang songs like "Roosevelt Oh Roosevelt." There was even a Jane Addams song book, which sold well at a few cents a copy to raise money for the campaign.

For all the excitement the Progressive party aroused, it still went down in defeat in November. With 6,293,000 votes, Woodrow Wilson, the Democratic candidate, swept most of the states. Roosevelt, on the other hand, received 4,119,000 votes and carried only six states.

Jane Addams was neither surprised, nor particularly dismayed. Shortly after the election, she told a reporter that she had expected Wilson to win from the start. The value of Roosevelt's candidacy, she said, lay in the wide publicity it had given to the need for social and industrial reforms. She was sure that Wilson as president would take up this reform program.

Addams's involvement with the Progressive party didn't, however, end with the campaign. She served on various committees and in general tried to keep the party's concern for social reform alive. But it soon became clear that Addams and other reformers wanted to go further than Roosevelt and his friends and advisers. At a meeting in New York in December, social workers active in the Progressive campaign agreed that Roosevelt had become suspicious of "the whole social worker crowd except Jane Addams." Since Roosevelt was afraid of Addams, she was the one they must depend on "to save the situation."

Instead, Addams gradually withdrew from the Progressive party. She did so because the party began to seem more and more like a lost cause. Also, she and other reformers were pleased by President Wilson's efforts in the area of social reform. For example, a child-labor law limiting the employment of young children in factories was passed. Another law provided for an eight-hour day for workers on the railroads.

At the same time, though, Addams kept up the fight for women's suffrage. On a trip to Europe and Egypt with Mary Smith in 1913, she made a point of attending the convention of the Woman's International Suffrage Association in Budapest, Hungary.

To reach Budapest, Addams boarded a Danube River steamer in the city of Vienna, Austria, and spent a pleasant day's journey with other women delegates from many different countries. The women on board took part in a long discussion on the use of force in the suffrage movement. A group of English suffragists made the case for more militant tactics. They supported the action of an Englishwoman who had recently hurled herself in front of the horses at the start of an important race to dramatize the cause of suffrage. Others argued against such tactics. They expressed the hope that once women got the vote, they would use it to prevent war.

Later Addams recalled, "Not a breath, not a tremor of the future, ruffled the polished surface of the Danube on that summer's day. There was no haunting [fear] that these bordering states within a year's time would be firing the opening shots of the most terrible war recorded in history."

8

Pacifist in Wartime

On a beautiful August morning in 1914, Jane Addams and Mary Smith saw something very surprising. A huge German liner lay at anchor in Frenchman's Bay near their cottage in Bar Harbor, Maine. The ship's captain had been several days out of New York when he learned war had started in Europe. He didn't want to return there because he feared his cargo of gold bullion would be captured. The sight of this large, out-of-place ship was in Addams's words "the first fantastic impression of that strange summer when we were so incredibly required to adjust our minds to a changed world."

The war was incredible to Addams because it upset all her theories. In *Newer Ideals of Peace*, for example, she had argued that the workingmen of the world would never accept war. She had also argued that women's motherly instincts would make them oppose war.

However, Addams hadn't reckoned on the bitter rivalries that had grown up among the nations of Europe. The various European countries competed for land and power in Africa and Asia as well as Europe. The fear and even hatred they felt for one another led them to build up huge armies. It also made them enter into rival alliances. Members of one alliance promised to support one another in case of attack. Thus a local crisis could spark a major war. The crisis came with the assassination of the heir to the throne of Austria-Hungary in June 1914. By August, the main powers of Europe were at war with one another. World War I, as it became known, pitted the Central Powers—Germany, Austria-Hungary, and the Ottoman Empire (modern-day Turkey)—against the Allied Powers—Britain, France, and Russia.

When the war broke out, President Woodrow Wilson declared that the United States would remain neutral—that is, it wouldn't take sides. Addams and many other Americans supported this policy and hoped and prayed the war would be over soon. In late September 1914, Addams went to New York to chair a meeting of other concerned social workers at Lillian Wald's Henry Street Settlement House. At the meeting, "the Henry Street group" was formed. This informal organization planned to explore ways to bring the war to a quick end and also to influence the peace settlement. Later the group organized the American Union Against Militarism, out of which came the American Civil Liberties Union (ACLU). Addams kept in touch with the Henry Street group and went to meetings when she could. But most of her energies were devoted to another peace organization.

The inspiration for this organization came not from Addams, but from abroad. Rosika Schwimmer was a thirty-seven-year-old Hungarian woman who supported women's rights and opposed war. Addams had met Schwimmer at the congress of the International Woman Suffrage Alliance in Budapest. When the fighting started, Schwimmer threw herself into peace efforts. She began circulating a petition. In it, she urged President Wilson to bring about a peaceful settlement of the conflict.

When Schwimmer arrived in the United States in September, Carrie Chapman Catt, an American suffrage leader, met her. Schwimmer had an interview with President Wilson. Then she set out on a speaking tour to enlist the support of American women for peace. Carrie Chapman Catt thought it would be a good idea to call a conference in Washington to bring all women who were pacifists—that is, opposed to war—together. She wrote to Addams, proposing they call the conference jointly. At first, Addams wasn't enthusiastic about the idea of a separate women's peace organization. But she agreed to go along with Catt's plan.

On January 10, 1915, about three thousand women jammed the ballroom of the New Willard Hotel in Washington, D.C. The group included many important and accomplished women besides Addams and Catt. Nevertheless, Addams presided at the sessions and delivered the keynote, or main, address. She became chairperson of the newly created Woman's Peace Party.

The women adopted a Peace Platform with eleven planks. They called for an immediate convention of neutral nations. This convention would try to help the warring countries settle their differences. The Woman's Peace Party hoped to win over first President Wilson, then the world to their program.

In February, Jane Addams received a telegram from Dr.

Aletta Jacobs. Dr. Jacobs was a dedicated suffragist and one of the first women doctors in Holland. She invited the Woman's Peace Party to send delegates to an international congress of women. The congress would meet at The Hague, Netherlands, from April 28 to May 1 that year. Addams was afraid the congress would turn out to be a waste of time and might even damage the cause of peace. But as both a pacifist and leader of American women, she felt she had to go.

On April 12, Addams, along with forty-one other delegates, set sail from New York on the *Noordam*, a Dutch ship. It was not pleasure cruise. That February, the German government had declared the waters around the British Isles a war zone. Neutral ships entering this zone ran the risk of being torpedoed by German submarines. The Germans took this action in self-defense. Britain was trying to starve Germany into submission by keeping ships with goods for Germany out of German ports. President Wilson had warned Germany that it would be held responsible for any loss of American ships or lives. But the Germans went ahead with their campaign of terror anyway. On May 7, 1915, several weeks after Addams and her party set sail, a German submarine torpedoed the British liner *Lusitania*, killing 1,189 people, including 128 Americans.

Meanwhile, the *Noordam* continued on its dangerous voyage. A few men, journalists mostly, were on board. But it was the women delegates who set the tone. They turned the ship into a classroom at sea with lectures three times a day on various aspects of the peace movement.

Tension ran high when the *Noordam* reached the English Channel. The ship was held up for four days there. The women were not allowed to land, to send messages, or to have anyone on board. At one point, a British gunboat came alongside and trained a machine gun on the ship, while two stowaways were removed. Addams did what she could to calm the women. She also appealed to the American ambassador to insist that the British government allow them to proceed. The ambassador telegraphed back that he could do nothing. Finally, the ship was released. The women delegates arrived at The Hague just two hours before the first session of the congress.

The mood of the women at The Hague was excited, if sometimes strained. Twelve nations were represented with over a thousand voting members. Sessions were conducted in several languages, and all sorts of resolutions were introduced, so there was some confusion. Yet Addams remained calm and unruffled in her role as chairperson. She won standing ovations whenever she rose to speak. Indeed, the only speaker more eloquent was Rosika Schwimmer.

The congress adopted a number of resolutions. It called for mild peace terms. It also called for the setting up of a permanent international congress and an international court of justice to make sure that war didn't break out again. There was to be no transfer of territory from one country to another without the consent of the people. Women were to be represented in both national and international politics.

The women also decided that delegates from the congress would present the resolutions to both the warring and neutral nations of Europe and to President Wilson. Jane Addams was selected to be one of these messengers. She thought the plan was "hopelessly melodramatic and absurd," but agreed to go.

Accompanied by Dr. Aletta Jacobs, Dr. Alice Hamilton, and another woman, Addams set out for the capitals of the

*Jane Addams (front row, second from the left) attended an
international meeting of women to demand an end to World War I.*

various nations that were at war. Another group, led by
Rosika Schwimmer, made its way to the capitals of the
neutral countries. For Addams and her party, it was a
strange and sometimes frightening trip. All around them
they would see signs of the war in the form of barricaded
cities, bombed-out buildings, and wounded soldiers. Yet for

the most part, they received a polite hearing when they presented their resolutions to the leaders of the warring nations.

The highlight of the trip was their interview with Prime Minister Karl von Stürgkh of Austria. Once they had finished their presentation, Addams started to apologize, "It perhaps seems to you very foolish that women should go about in this way...." At this, the minister banged his fist on the table and cried: "Foolish? Not at all. These are the first sensible words that have been uttered in this room for ten months."

When their separate missions were over, the two groups of delegates were to meet in Amsterdam, the Netherlands. There they were to discuss the next step in organizing a conference of neutral nations to stop the war. But at the end of June, Jane Addams decided to return to the United States. She hadn't been eager to go on the mission in the first place. Now she felt she could do more for the cause of peace in her own country. Also, she was tired of traveling and longed to be with Mary Smith at Bar Harbor, enjoying a needed rest.

Rosika Schwimmer was furious with Addams for leaving. She had never quite trusted Addams and called her "slippery Jane," because she said it was hard to pin Addams down to a particular position.

When her ship docked in New York on July 5, Addams was met by a group of fifty people wearing white ribbons that said "Welcome Jane Addams." Four days later, a large audience gathered at Carnegie Hall to hear her describe The Hague meeting and her visits to the various European capitals. Addams said that in all the warring countries a revolt against war was going on. Everywhere they went, she and her party had heard people say that it was an old man's war, and that the young men who were fighting and dying weren't those who wanted the war.

Addams gave several examples of soldiers' reluctance to fight. Her final example had to do with bayonet charges. People in all the countries they had visited told her that soldiers had to be given a stimulant of either alcohol or a drug before they would take part in a bayonet charge.

This last remark stirred up a storm of outrage. "Troops Drink-Crazed, says Miss Addams," shrieked the headlines the next day. A few days later, Richard Harding Davis, a popular novelist and war correspondent, wrote a letter to *The New York Times*. He attacked Addams and defended the honor and courage of the soldiers. Newspapers all over the country picked up the story and Davis's letter, with most taking his side. Addams also received numerous angry letters about the speech. The attacks hurt. She tried to explain and defend her remark, but most people refused to listen.

Addams also failed to persuade President Wilson to call a conference of neutral nations to stop the fighting. She saw Wilson in July and again in the fall. But neither her visits nor those of other peace leaders won a definite commitment from the president.

That fall, an impatient Rosika Schwimmer tried a different tactic. Schwimmer heard that the millionaire automobile manufacturer, Henry Ford, had said he would be willing to spend half his fortune to shorten the war by just one day. She went to see Ford and persuaded him to charter a ship, the *Oscar II*. This ship would carry delegates to an unofficial peace conference overseas.

The Ford Peace Ship quickly became a target of ridicule by the press. Addams herself was dismayed by the showmanship involved and by the guest list, which included many with no experience in the peace movement. Most of the distinguished citizens invited refused to go. Many of Addams's friends urged her to decline, too. Yet Addams felt her presence on board the *Oscar II* and at the neutral conference would help the cause of peace.

Nevertheless, on December 4, 1915, the *Oscar II* sailed without Addams. Seriously ill with pneumonia, she was confined to a Chicago hospital bed. Perhaps it was just as well. The Ford Peace Ship was a disaster from the start. Rosika Schwimmer angered many on board with her bossy ways. Also, Henry Ford's failure to make clear exactly who was going to get the money he had promised caused confusion and resentment. Addams herself created problems by trying to keep the Ford Peace Ship distinct from the Woman's Peace Party. Dr. Aletta Jacobs and other women peace advocates in Europe misunderstood Addams's message. They refused to have anything to do with the Ford Peace Ship. Ford got fed up and pulled out of the project on Christmas Eve, without fulfilling his pledge "to get the boys home for Christmas."

Although Addams hadn't gone on the Ford Peace Ship, people used it to attack her anyway. Many newspaper accounts suggested that her illness was imaginary and a convenient excuse for not sailing on the peace ship. Theodore Roosevelt, Addams's former partner in the Progressive crusade, joined in the attack. He denounced Addams as "one of the shrieking sisterhood," as "poor bleeding Jane," and as a "Bull Mouse."

Despite these attacks and her own poor health, Addams continued with her peace work. In January 1916, she testified before the Military Affairs Committee of the U.S. House of Representatives. She argued against the buildup of the army and navy in case the nation went to war. She also met with President Wilson again and was cheered when he drew out a copy of the women's congress resolutions, given him six months before. She could tell that the document had been handled and read. Wilson told her he had studied the resolutions and considered them the best proposals anyone had yet made. Still, he wouldn't commit himself to act on them.

Weakened by the trip to Washington, Addams went to California to recuperate. She returned to Chicago in April. But almost immediately she showed alarming symptoms that were diagnosed as tuberculosis of the kidneys. She underwent surgery to remove one of her kidneys. For the next two years, she was a semi-invalid.

Addams spent the summer and early fall of 1916 at Bar Harbor, trying to rest, but also working on a new book. Published later that year, the book was called *The Long Road of Woman's Memory*. After *The Spirit of Youth and City Streets*, it was Addams's favorite of all her books. The subject wasn't her personal memory, but the "race memories" of all women. Addams believed that these race memories were passed down from one generation of women to the next in the myths and fairy tales mothers told their daughters. Through myths and fairy tales, Addams wrote, women had first begun to challenge savagery and war.

That summer and fall, another presidential campaign took place. Both Wilson and the Republican candidate, Charles Evans Hughes, tried to secure Addams's support. She finally decided to back Wilson. She was pleased by his efforts in the area of social justice and hopeful that he would still try to end the war. After Addams made public her support of Wilson, the president wrote her a warm note of thanks. Then after his reelection, he invited her to dinner at the White House.

In January 1917, Wilson seemed to justify the faith that Addams and others in the peace movement had placed in him. In his famous "Peace Without Victory" speech, he called for an end to the war before either side had achieved victory. He also proposed an international organization to maintain world peace.

But Wilson had waited too long. At the end of January, Germany announced that its submarines would once again attack the ships of neutral nations as well as those of its enemies. Earlier, Wilson had threatened to break off relations with Germany if it didn't stop sinking neutral ships. Now he made good this threat.

Addams tried desperately to keep the nation out of the war. She helped form an Emergency Peace Federation. This organization held demonstrations at the White House and launched a letter-writing campaign. She also had one final interview with Wilson. But the president wouldn't listen to her appeal. Early in April 1917, he delivered a war message to Congress, and Congress voted to declare war. The United States had finally entered into the battles of World War I.

Addams was now faced with an agonizing choice. Should she support the war? Or should she remain a pacifist? If she chose the first course, she would be going along with most of her friends—people like Mary Smith and Louise Bowen, as well as many who had been active in the peace movement. On the other hand, she would disappoint the many European women who looked to her as a leading American opponent of the war. Worse still, she would disappoint herself. She had worked too hard and suffered too much ridicule and abuse to give up now. If she did, she doubted she would be able to hold her head up high again.

The very nature of World War I may have influenced Adams's decision. She was against all wars. But this one was particularly horrible. For almost three years now, soldiers on both sides had faced each other along miles of muddy, rat-infested ditches. This type of trench warfare was especially deadly. Soldiers had to wear gas masks to keep the poison gas that was used from blistering their skin, burning their eyes, and destroying their lungs. They had to endure days of constant shelling. Then they were ordered "over the top" only to be caught in a tangle of barbed wire and mowed down by machine-gun fire. On one day alone, nearly 20,000 British soldiers were killed. Before the war was over, 10 million soldiers on both sides would be killed. Millions of civilians would die from disease, starvation, and revolutions that grew out of the war.

A few of Addams's friends and co-workers like Lillian Wald and Dr. Alice Hamilton stood with her in opposing the war. Though she disagreed with Addams's position, Mary Smith remained personally loyal. But with the overwhelming majority in favor of the war, Addams strongly felt "the destroying effect of aloneness."

She tried to explain and defend her stand in a speech entitled "Patriotism and Pacifists in Wartime." Pacifists were not cowards or traitors, Addams argued. Rather they wanted their country to make a strong effort "to lead all nations of the earth into an organized international life worthy of civilized men."

Addams gave this speech at the Chicago City Club and at the University of Chicago. At both places, she was received with coolness, though not outright hostility. Then in June 1917, she spoke at the First Congregational Church in Evanston, Illinois. When she had finished speaking, Judge Orrin Carter of the Illinois Supreme Court jumped to his feet.

"I have always been a friend of Miss Addams," Judge Carter said when questions were called for, "but..."

"The 'but,'" Jane Addams broke in lightly, "sounds as if you were going to break with me."

"I am going to break with you. Anything which tends to cast doubt on the justice of our cause in the present war is very unfortunate. No pacifist measures should be taken until the war is over," Judge Carter said almost angrily.

"Perhaps my subject was an unfortunate one to be discussed at this time," replied Miss Addams slowly, "but surely that should be referred to the committee which invited me to speak."

With that, the meeting came to an abrupt end. A few people wrote praising Addams's speech. But most were highly critical and even insulting. One man called Addams "an awful ass" and attacked her speeches as "unpatriotic and pro-German."

In fact, Addams had lost her audience. Only a few peace groups invited her to speak, and magazines no longer wanted to print her articles. Since many social workers disagreed with her position on the war, they stopped writing her for advice. In a public statement, Mary Kingsbury Simkhovitch, president of the National Federation of Settlements, said: "It has been very painful to many of us who hold Miss Addams in deep affection and wholly respect her to find that we cannot think or act in unison with her."

At Hull House itself, Addams found herself largely

alone. Most of the male residents supported the war, and more of the women were for than against it. Eleven members of the Hull House Boys' Band, along with their bandmaster, enlisted as a group and were sent to France. All soldiers in the district came to Hull House for their last meal "at home." Afterward, they said their farewells in the Hull House courtyard.

Hull House was also the place where immigrants in the neighborhood came to register for the draft. As Addams described the scene:

"In they came heavily, one man after another. . . . I knew most of them. . . . I said nothing beyond the morning's greeting, but one of them stopped to speak to me. He had been in the Hull House citizenship classes. . . . He spoke from the bitterness of his heart:

"'I have you to thank if I am sent over to Europe to fight. I went into the citizenship class because you asked me to. If I hadn't my papers now I would be exempted.'"

Addams not only felt alone, but useless. She gave up trying to speak about the war. Even so, she learned that the Department of Justice was keeping a close watch on her.

Early in 1918, however, Addams found a job she could do without betraying her pacifist principles. The previous summer, a federal Department of Food Administration had been created. Herbert Hoover, a businessman who had successfully managed food relief in war-torn Belgium, was put in charge. Addams was impressed by Hoover's appeal to Americans to save food and grow more crops to keep Europeans from starving. She went to work for the Food Administration, speaking at women's clubs, public schools, and public meetings throughout the country.

In her talks, Addams said that nations needed to

cooperate to solve the food crisis. She wondered if perhaps the need to work the land and produce food was a basic human impulse. This would explain why Russian peasant soldiers had quit fighting when the Russian Revolution broke out in 1917.

Addams was also interested in the connection between women and "bread labor." After poring over ancient myths about food, she decided that it was woman's desire to grow food for her children that made her settle in one place and become domestic. She hoped women would expand their ancient role as "breadgivers" to their families to include the entire world.

People listened to Addams when she talked about food, as they had not when she tried to speak of peace. Some even hailed her as a figure from one of the myths she described— a sort of Corn or Earth Mother. By the time the armistice, or truce, ending the war, was signed on November 11, 1918, Addams had regained some of her former reputation. Not everyone was ready to proclaim her a saint. But at least she was viewed as less of a villain.

However, this would soon change, as the nation entered the difficult postwar period.

9

A Dangerous Radical

With the war over, Jane Addams again threw her energies into the women's peace movement. The delegates to the 1915 Hague conference had agreed to hold their next meeting at the same time and place as the official peace conference. But Paris instead of a location in a neutral country was chosen for the official conference. So the women decided to have their meeting at Zurich, Switzerland. That way, delegates from Germany, Austria, and the other defeated nations could more easily attend.

Early in April 1919, Addams sailed for Europe with the rest of the American delegation. Its members included Alice Hamilton, Lillian Wald, and Florence Kelley. Emily Balch, an economics professor from Wellesley College who had been active in the peace movement, was also in the party. So was Jeanette Rankin, a congresswoman from Montana who had voted against the U.S. entry into the war.

Arriving in France in late April, the women spent a few days in Paris interviewing officials at the peace conference. Then Addams, Hamilton, Rankin, and Wald went on a five-day tour of ruined battlefields for the American Red Cross. Many of the dead were still unburied. The women saw American soldiers digging rows of graves for corpses that were piled in trucks.

Addams wanted to find the grave of her oldest nephew, John Linn. An Episcopalian minister, Linn had served as chaplain to an artillery unit. He had been killed in the Argonne Forest in France while passing out chocolate to the men under heavy fire. Before his death, he had written to Addams: "I shall probably be killed, but if I am not I shall not come back. There will be too much to do over here that is worth while, and I should not like the thought of having come to Europe only for uselessness." Addams found his grave after a long search through muddy graveyards under a cold, driving rain.

The suffering caused by the war was evident even in neutral Switzerland. The day of her arrival in Zurich, Addams was walking along a street when she met one of the Austrian women who had been a delegate to The Hague congress. The woman was "so shrunken and changed" that Addams hardly recognized her as the beautiful woman of three years before. Not only was the woman very thin, "but her face and artist's hands were covered with rough red blotches due to the long use of soap substitutes, giving her a cruelly scalded appearance."

Despite such glimpses of the tragic effects of the war, Addams was happy to be with a large group of like-minded women again. About 150 women from sixteen countries attended the congress. The first thing they did was pass a

Millions of soldiers and civilians died in World War I. Even more people, about 21 million, died in the flu epidemic of 1918, which war conditions helped spread.

resolution condemning the widespread hunger and disease left by the war. They urged the Paris Peace Conference to end the blockade that was keeping food and other necessities from the starving, ill peoples of the defeated nations. Their resolution was wired to President Wilson in Paris.

The women had every reason to believe that Wilson would be sympathetic. In January 1918, the president had made a speech outlining the Fourteen Points that he considered necessary for a just and lasting peace. Several of Wilson's "Points" were based on the resolutions passed by the women's congress in 1915. They included the peaceful settlement of disputes and the creation of an international peacekeeping organization, the League of Nations. But now Wilson wired back that while he personally supported the women's request, he doubted he could get the other leaders of the victorious powers to support it. The trouble was that the Allies weren't interested in "a peace without victory." They were determined to crush Germany and its allies.

This became clear to Addams and the other delegates when they received an advance copy of the peace treaty. They were stunned and horrified by the harsh terms imposed on Germany and its allies. Not only was Germany completely disarmed, but it had to pay reparations—large sums of money—to the nations that had won the war. The delegates were convinced that the treaty contained the seeds of future war. The congress was one of the first bodies to review the treaty. Its criticisms anticipated those that would be both made and accepted much later.

Addams and the other members of the congress were pleased that the treaty provided for a League of Nations. But they worried that the league would prove too weak to be effective. They decided to set up their own permanent organization—the Women's International League for Peace and Freedom (WIL). Addams was elected president, and Emily Balch, secretary-treasurer.

The choice of Addams as president was no surprise to anyone. She had led the sessions with skill and ease, suggesting compromises and soothing hurt feelings when necessary. In her closing speech, Addams called on the delegates to use "moral energy" to "heal the world and bring it back to a normal condition."

From Zurich, Addams returned to Paris to give President Wilson the resolutions passed by the congress. While there, she met with Herbert Hoover. He helped her with another undertaking. She and Alice Hamilton had been invited by a group of English and American Quakers to make a trip into Germany. They were to investigate the needs of the German people and make arrangements for distributing food and clothing collected by the Society of Friends.

Addams and Hamilton had a long wait before they could start on this errand of mercy. The peace treaty hadn't been signed, and U.S. officials didn't want American women inside Germany when there was still a chance that Germany might not sign. Finally, though, they were granted special visas and arrived in Berlin on July 7, 1919.

Addams and Hamilton were appalled by the thousands of starving children they saw in Berlin, Frankfort, Leipzig, and other German cities. At Leipzig, they visited a playground where more than six hundred children spent the day and were given a midday meal. Each child got a pint of "war soup"—hot water into which wheat or rye flour had been stirred, along with a little dried vegetable. The women also noted a great increase in such diseases as tuberculosis and typhus, which had been under control before the war.

Upon her return to the United States in August, Addams took up the cause of these sick, starving German children. She made speeches and worked to raise money to feed them. Yet throughout the country, she was attacked as being pro-German and un-American. In one city, she was heckled for forty-five minutes before she was allowed to speak.

The attacks against Addams became especially violent in 1920. At this time, she protested the Justice Department's treatment of foreign-born radicals. The war had bred an increased fear and hatred of foreigners. The Russian Revolution of 1917 added to this ugly mood. The revolution brought the Bolsheviks, called Reds, to power. They set up a

Communist government, in which all the farms and factories were owned and controlled by the government. They also called upon workers around the world to rise up and overthrow their governments.

Many Americans became convinced that a Communist plot to take over the U.S. government was under way. The Justice Department arrested and jailed thousands of people during the so-called Red Scare. Eventually, the panic died down. But Addams and others who had defended the rights of the radicals remained suspect throughout most of the decade.

The year 1920 saw the publication of the Lusk Report. This was a four-volume study of radical activities, prepared by the New York State Legislature. The report linked peace organizations, women's groups, and social reformers with communism and bolshevism. Because of her work as a reformer and pacifist, Addams's name appeared frequently in the report. This led many to brand her a Communist and even denounce her as "the most dangerous woman in America."

The Lusk Report was soon followed by the so-called spider-web charts. One column contained a list of names of prominent people such as Jane Addams, Florence Kelley, Julia Lathrop, and Eugene Debs. In the other column was a list of "radical" organizations like the American Civil Liberties Union, founded in 1920. A tangle of lines connected individuals to the various organizations to which they belonged—hence the name spider-web chart. Addams's name stood out on these lists because it came at the beginning of the alphabet. Also, she belonged to many supposedly radical organizations.

Among the groups that attacked Addams were the American Legion and the Daughters of the American

Revolution (DAR). Addams had been elected to the DAR in 1895 and had been made an honorary member in 1900. But now the organization turned violently against her. The attacks wounded Addams more than she liked to admit. To friends, she confessed, "You know, I am really getting old. I find it is not as easy to love my enemies as it used to be."

Still, Addams kept up her work for the Women's International League (WIL). The WIL had set up its main office in Geneva, Switzerland. Emily Balch, the secretary-treasurer, ran the day-to-day operations. But Addams raised five hundred dollars a month to help keep the organization going. As president, she played an important role at the WIL's various congresses. In 1921, she journeyed to Vienna, Austria, to preside over the third congress of the WIL.

Addams was in her glory while abroad. But upon her return home she met with difficulties and disappointment. In June 1922, social workers gathered at Providence, Rhode Island. They planned to elect a fiftieth anniversary president of their conference. Some of Addams's friends such as Julia Lathrop and Alice Hamilton pushed her candidacy. Addams herself very much wanted the presidency. But it soon became clear that too many people opposed Addams because of her stand against the war. So she withdrew her name. The presidency went to a less controversial social worker.

Even more painful was her failure to win the Nobel Peace Prize. Alfred Nobel, a wealthy Swedish engineer and philanthropist, had set up a fund for this prize. Each year, beginning in 1901, it was awarded to the person who had done the most for world peace. Throughout the decade, Addams was nominated nearly every year for the award, but with no success.

She was no longer in demand as a speaker either.

Recalled Maude Royden, a British doctor and friend of Addams, "How well I remember, when I spoke in America in 1922 and 1923, the silence that greeted the name of Jane Addams! The few faithful who tried to applaud only made the silence more depressing."

Also, fewer people bought books by Addams. Her income from both the sales of her books and from lectures dropped sharply. In 1922 when *Peace and Bread in Time of War* came out, it hardly attracted the readership that Addams's previous books had.

Unwelcome in her own country, Addams began spending more and more time abroad. In 1922, she traveled to The Hague to attend a Conference for a New Peace. The conference had been called by the WIL, but it drew representatives of more than a hundred organizations from twenty countries. Afterward, Jane Addams and Mary Smith journeyed to East Asia and around the world. They visited Burma, India, the Philippines, Korea, China, and Japan.

In India, Addams tried to visit the great leader Mahatma Gandhi. She was fascinated by his use of nonviolent tactics in the struggle for independence from Britain. Gandhi organized protest marches and fasts. He urged his followers not to obey unjust laws or use British products. But Addams never got a chance to talk to Gandhi because he only received two visitors every six months, and one of these was his wife.

In Japan, Addams had an emergency operation to remove a breast tumor that turned out not to be cancerous. She left just a few days before a terrible earthquake leveled Tokyo. Enthusiastic crowds greeted Addams everywhere she went. At one place in Japan, five thousand schoolchildren waving flags hailed her arrival.

In December 1923, Addams summed up her impressions of her world tour in a Christmas message to the women of the world. She was concerned that there wasn't enough active goodwill in the world "to accomplish the healing of the nations." She noted that the countries of Europe were divided and lived in a state of fear. The United States, meanwhile, had retreated into a policy of isolation from Europe. (It had not, as Wilson, Addams and others hoped, joined the League of Nations.) Another alarming sign was that nations like China and Japan were following Europe's example by building up their armies and navies. Still, Addams hoped that peace might yet be the result.

The following May, eighty-five delegates from nineteen countries came to Washington for the fourth congress of the Women's International League. Once again, Addams presided. But this time, she found herself in an embarassing position. She had to apologize for the unfriendly way the congress was received by American newspapers and various patriotic groups.

The congress was followed by a two weeks' summer school in Chicago. A special railway car, dubbed the "Pax Special," was hired to transport the delegates from Washington to Chicago. The plan was to hold meetings on behalf of peace at various towns and cities along the way. However, some of the meetings had to be canceled because of protests by the DAR, the American Legion, and other organizations.

During the next two years, Addams continued to travel outside the country. In 1925, she spent a month vacationing in Mexico. In 1926, she went to Dublin, Ireland, for the fifth congress of the WIL. There, however, she suffered a heart attack. She recovered, but the attack left her with a "bad heart."

Despite this serious ailment and frequent bouts of seasickness, Addams loved to travel. She enjoyed staying at elegant hotels, eating at good restaurants, and being entertained by famous and important people. Moreover, she found her work for the WIL very rewarding.

Indeed, the time and energy Addams had formerly given to Hull House now went to the Women's International League. Addams spent less and less time at the settlement house. Even when she was in Chicago, she usually stayed at Mary Smith's home rather than at Hull House.

By this time, many of the settlement's "old guard" had departed. Florence Kelley was in New York, serving as general secretary of the National Consumers' League. Julia Lathrop had retired to Rockford after ten years in Washington as head of the federal Children's Bureau. Alice Hamilton was in Boston, teaching at Harvard Medical School. Ellen Starr had entered a Catholic convent.

Able residents remained at Hull House. But there was no one to tease Addams or spur her to action. Also, some of the younger men and women secretly resented both Addams and her highly personal way of managing Hull House without a thought to what would happen after she was gone.

Addams herself was disappointed with the direction the settlement movement was taking in the 1920s. Many settlements had turned their backs on reform, and many were in financial trouble. It was hard for them to recruit able young people. Social work itself had changed. When Jane Addams and Ellen Starr had founded Hull House, social work wasn't an organized profession. There were no set guidelines for them to follow. They simply did whatever seemed right and necessary. Now, however, social workers had to worry about meeting professional standards. Also, their interests had changed. The new generation of social workers was more concerned with treating individual cases involving emotional or mental disorders than with social reform.

In fact, Addams had little sympathy for or understanding of the entire younger generation. She disapproved of the new freedom in relations between men and women. She also disapproved of the so-called flappers—young women who broke with tradition by wearing short dresses and bright lipstick and rouge and by smoking and drinking in public.

Addams further rejected the younger women's demand for equality. Naturally, she had rejoiced when the Nineteenth Amendment, giving women the vote, had gone into effect in 1920. But she was against the Equal Rights Amendment (ERA) to the Constitution that was put forward at this time. This amendment read: "Equality of rights under the law shall not be denied or abridged by the United States on account of sex." Addams and others like Florence Kelley and Alice Hamilton had worked long and hard for special laws to protect working women. They were afraid that these laws would become meaningless if Congress passed an amendment declaring that women had equal rights with men.

Addams and other social workers did, however, support the Eighteenth Amendment. This amendment prohibited the manufacture and sale of alcohol anywhere in the United States. Addams deplored the crime and violence that came as a result of Prohibition. But otherwise she felt the law was a good idea. She had never touched alcohol herself and disapproved of drinking by working-class and upper-class people alike.

In these ways, Addams was out of step with the times.

Where once she had led the way, now she seemed a throwback to an earlier, simpler era. She no longer served as a role model for college women.

But old friends remained loyal and defended Addams against the continuing attacks. They organized a huge dinner in her honor in Chicago in January 1927. At this dinner, Charles E. Merriam, professor of politics at Chicago University, hailed Addams as a "statesman without portfolio, a professor without a chair, a guiding woman in a man-made world."

Two years later, in 1929, Addams went to what was to be her last WIL congress in Prague, Czechoslovakia. At this congress, she resigned as president. She was almost seventy, her health wasn't good, and she was tired. Still, many begged her not to resign. One European woman said that the league was so "deeply connected" with Addams's personality that she couldn't imagine it continuing without her. Never one to disappoint those who believed in her, Addams agreed to remain honorary president for life.

10

Saint Jane Again

As a new decade began, Jane Addams turned seventy. A splendid dinner was given in her honor at Louise Bowen's house in Bar Harbor, Maine. The year 1930 also saw the publication of the sequel to Addams's autobiography, *The Second Twenty Years at Hull House*. Addams had worked on this book throughout most of the 1920s. Because it dealt with the painful years of the war and its aftermath, she had trouble writing it. For this reason perhaps, the book turned out to be much less personal and compelling than the earlier volume. One reviewer commented that reading *The Second Twenty Years at Hull House* "makes one a little homesick for the days before the war when Jane Addams was a sort of national saint and we all believed in ideals."

Yet in the last years of her life many people once again considered Addams as a national saint. Changed conditions had much to do with this. In the 1930s, the nation was in the grips of an economic crisis so severe it became known as the Great Depression.

The trouble began when the stock market crashed in 1929, wiping out tens of thousands of investors. As the panic spread, thousands of banks closed, businesses failed, and by 1932, 12 million people were out of work. Many of the jobless took to the roads, wandering from town to town in search of work. In cities the homeless sought shelter by building shacks of wooden crates and pieces of metal. Hungry families waited for hours in breadlines and in front of soup kitchens. Some parents even searched in garbage pails to keep their children from starving.

Against this grim backdrop, Jane Addams's work for the poor seemed meaningful again. So, too, did her work for peace now that there were rumblings of war from abroad.

Oddly enough, the first of many awards that Addams received in her last years was the Medal of Military Merit from the government of Greece. It was for her services to the Greek Army during World War I. These services, Addams discovered, consisted of having allowed the Greek Americans of the Hull House neighborhood to use Bowen Hall for military drill before going over to join the Greek Army. She preferred to think the award expressed the affection her Greek-American neighbors felt for her.

The shift of public opinion in Addams's favor was evident at a Conference on the Cause and Cure of War that she attended in Washington in January 1931. When a representative of the DAR tried to heckle Addams, the audience laughed at the heckler instead of booing Addams.

From Washington, Addams traveled to Arizona to escape the worst of the Chicago winter. While there, she learned of another award. *Good Housekeeping Magazine* had named her first among "America's Twelve Greatest Women." An all-male jury made the selection. Addams commented: "One of the committee formerly regarded me as a traitor, and I'm quite sure that two at least of the others had never heard of me before this 'contest.'"

Other lists followed. One list of the "seven greatest Americans of all time" included Jane Addams; the inventor Thomas A. Edison; Henry Ford; George Washington; and Abraham Lincoln.

That year also, Addams won two awards, each of which was worth five thousand dollars. One was from a popular magazine, *The Pictorial Review*, "to the woman who in her special field has made the most distinguished contribution to American life." The other was the C. Carey Thomas Award given by Bryn Mawr College to a woman of great achievement. Addams was only the second woman to receive this award, the first having been the longtime president of the college, C. Carey Thomas herself. Addams went to Bryn Mawr to receive the award, accompanied by one of her grandnieces who was a graduate of the college.

Not long afterward, Addams attended her own fiftieth graduation anniversary at Rockford. Over the years she had kept in close touch with the college. In 1883, just two years after she had graduated, she had been appointed a member of the college's board of trustees—quite an honor for one as young as she. And when she had come into money of her own after her father's death, she had made a gift of a thousand dollars to the Rockford College library. The money was to be used to add to the college's scanty collection of scientific books. Now returning to the college for the celebration, Addams found eight of her sixteen classmates alive and in attendance at the event.

In the fall, Addams went to Washington to present a petition in favor of international disarmament to President Herbert Hoover. She was enthusiastically received.

Then late in November 1931, the long-awaited news came. Addams received a telegram informing her that along with Dr. Nicholas Murray Butler, the president of Columbia University, she had won the Nobel Peace Prize for that year. Of course, she was delighted. Yet almost a decade had passed since Addams had first begun to hope for this award. So its coming now must have seemed somewhat of a letdown. Also, she had to share it with Butler. He had been active in the peace movement before World War I. But Butler had supported the United States' entry into the war. He had even criticized Wilson for not coming to the aid of the Allies sooner. One of Addams's friends wired: "Three cheers this is certainly good news although I wish Nick might have been eliminated." A few thought it should have been the other way around. But most of the same newspapers that had attacked Addams during and after the war now heaped praise on her.

Shortly after Addams received notification of the award, she underwent an operation to remove a tumor. Her recovery was slow. By early spring, she was still too weak to attend either the next WIL congress in Grenoble, France, or go to Oslo, Norway, to make her Nobel Prize speech.

Addams gave her Nobel Prize money, approximately $16,000, to the WIL. The $5,000 each from Bryn Mawr and *The Pictorial Review* went to help the unemployed in the Hull House neighborhood. In a depression year, this was a great deal of money. Still, it was hardly enough to stem the tide of misery.

Addams was deeply saddened by the hard times. She

During her last years, Jane Addams regained much of the public's affection, despite her controversial and pioneering activities.

was particularly concerned about the effects of the Great Depression on the very young and the very old. To help the elderly, she pushed for a system of old age pensions. As chairperson of the Illinois Committee for Old Age Security, she campaigned vigorously for pension bills before the state legislature.

In the election of 1932, Addams supported President Herbert Hoover for reelection, even though she realized he hadn't done enough soon enough to fight the depression. But when Franklin Roosevelt became president instead, she gave him her wholehearted support. She was happy when he chose a former Hull House resident, Frances Perkins, to be secretary of labor. She herself accepted a position on the Chicago advisory committee of the Housing Division of the Public Works Administration (PWA) under the direction of another old friend, Harold Ickes.

Addams was thrilled by the PWA and other programs of the "New Deal" that Roosevelt promised depression-weary Americans. The PWA used federal money to build roads, government buildings, and other public projects. In Chicago, the federal government cleared out three large slum areas not far from Hull House. Projects like these resulted in improvements while at the same time providing work for the jobless. Other New Deal programs gave direct relief to the needy, tried to help businesses recover, and sought to reform conditions in the economy that had caused the depression. All in all, Addams found the first years of the New Deal "a wonderful time to live" despite the suffering that went along with continued unemployment.

Events abroad troubled Addams, however. She was horrified by the Japanese invasion of Manchuria, and by the rise to power in Germany of Adolf Hitler, the leader of the

National Socialist, or Nazi, party. She was also sharply critical of the United States for refusing to disarm.

Nevertheless, Addams remained hopeful that peace could be preserved by moral force, international trade agreements, and the eventual end of warlike thinking. As she said at one point, "A great Kingdom of Peace lies close at hand ready to come into being, if we would but turn toward it." Although unable to attend WIL congresses, she continued to raise money for the organization and corresponded with women peace leaders throughout the world.

In the winter of 1933–34, Addams was confined to her bed at Mary Smith's house for four months with bronchitis and heart trouble. Mary Smith herself became ill with bronchitis, which developed into pneumonia. In March 1934, she died.

Addams had lost other old friends before this. Julia Lathrop and Florence Kelley had both died two years earlier. But Mary Smith's death was the greatest blow of all. Later Addams told her nephew, "I suppose I could have willed my heart to stop beating, and I longed to relax into doing that, but the thought of what she had been to me for so long kept me from being cowardly."

For more than forty years, Mary Smith had been Addams's closest friend and almost constant companion. The two women had traveled together, spent summers at Bar Harbor together, and when apart, exchanged long, affectionate letters. Addams had even written a poem about Mary and her "delivering love." Addams's deep attachment to Mary Smith stood in contrast to her relationships with others. She was kind to people, but kept her distance.

Addams took a long time to recover from both Mary Smith's death and her own illness. But by March 1935, she was well enough to travel to Berkeley, California, to receive, along with Frances Perkins and Herbert Hoover, an honorary degree from the University of California. (The Berkeley degree was one of many Addams received in her last years. Other honorary degrees came from Northwestern, the University of Chicago, Swarthmore, Rollins, Knox, and Mt. Holyoke colleges.)

April found Addams back in Chicago, spending her afternoons at Hull House and even putting in an appearance at a benefit concert for the Hull House Music School. At the beginning of May, she traveled to Washington, D.C., to attend the twentieth anniversary of the Women's International League.

Addams was the guest of honor at this event. Although she didn't feel up to the afternoon reception given by First Lady Eleanor Roosevelt, she did go to the dinner that night. Twelve hundred people gathered in the Willard Hotel ballroom to hear Secretary of the Interior Harold Ickes hail Addams as "the truest American" he had ever known and Eleanor Roosevelt praise her as "a pioneer who was still pioneering."

The next day, Addams had lunch with a number of women who had accompanied her to the first meeting of the Women's International League at The Hague twenty years before. Then she went to a broadcasting studio to take part in a radio "peace program" involving a link-up with speakers in London, Tokyo, Moscow, and Paris. She concluded the program with these words:

"The Women's International League joins a long procession of those who have endeavored for hundreds of years, to substitute law for war, political processes for brute force,

Jane Addams shortly before her death in 1935.

and we are grateful to our friends from various parts of the world who recognize at least our sincerity in this effort."

It was her last public address. Several days later, she was stricken with severe abdominal pain and went into the hospital. An operation revealed unsuspected but long-standing cancer. She died on May 21, 1935.

People all over the country and throughout the world expressed deep sorrow at the news of Addams's death. Thousands of men, women, and children filed solemnly past her casket as she lay in state at Bowen Hall at Hull House. And thousands jammed the Hull House courtyard, where the funeral was held. The Hull House Woman's Club, the Hull House Dramatic Association, and the graduates of the Boys Club formed a guard of honor. Boys and girls from the various clubs served as ushers. After the funeral, Addams's body was taken to Cedarville, where she was buried in the Addams lot in the cemetery started by her father.

In the following weeks, numerous tributes to Addams appeared in newspapers and magazines, and in speeches made at memorial services. In death as in life, many hailed her as a saintly figure who gave up a life of ease to live among the poor. Yet others looked beyond her obvious goodness to her greatness. Emily Balch, who succeeded Addams as president of the WIL, called her a leader like George Washington and Abraham Lincoln. "She was a constructive organizer and builder with judgment of extraordinary penetration and sureness, an original intellect...."

Journalist and author Walter Lippmann agreed that Addams was not only good but great. "She had compassion without condescension," he wrote. "She had infinite sympathy for common things without forgetfulness of those that are uncommon."

These qualities shone through in Jane Addams's pioneering efforts to promote peace as well as her work for the poor. In both areas, she laid important foundations for future generations to build upon.

Important Dates

1860 Jane Addams is born on September 6 in Cedarville, Illinois, the daughter of John and Sarah Addams.

1863 Jane Addams's mother dies.

1868 John Addams marries Anna Haldeman, a widow with two sons.

1877–1881 Jane Addams attends Rockford Seminary.

1881 John Addams dies.

1881–1882 Jane Addams studies at the Woman's Medical College, Philadelphia.

1887–1888 Addams makes a trip to Europe with Ellen Starr and another friend.

1889 Addams and Ellen Starr move into Hull House in Chicago on September 18.

1890 Julia Lathrop and Mary Rozet Smith come to Hull House.

1891 Addams and Mary Kenny found the Jane Club, a cooperative boardinghouse for working girls. Florence Kelley joins the group of residents at Hull House.

1893 Lobbying by Addams and other Hull House residents leads to the passage of the first factory law in Illinois. Hull House offers shelter to homeless women during the depression of that year.

1894 Addams joins in the effort to settle the Pullman Strike. Her oldest sister, Mary, dies.

1895 Addams is appointed garbage inspector for the Nineteenth Ward. She becomes ill with typhoid fever.

1896 Addams and other Hull House residents launch their first campaign to defeat ward boss, Johnny Powers.

1899 Hull House residents lobby for a law that sets up the first juvenile court in the United States.

1901 Addams defends the anarchist Abraham Isaak when he is arrested following the assassination of President McKinley.

1902 Addams's first book, *Democracy and Social Ethics*, is published.

1905–1909 Addams serves on the Chicago School Board.

1907 Addams's second book, *Newer Ideals of Peace*, is published.

1910 Addams publishes her autobiography, *Twenty Years at Hull House*.

1912 Addams takes part in the campaign of the Progressive party for the presidency.

1913 Addams attends the convention of the Woman's International Suffrage Association in Budapest, Hungary.

1915 Addams presides at the convention of the Woman's Peace Party in Washington, D.C. She goes to The Hague for the first congress of the Women's International League for Peace and Freedom.

1917 The United States enters World War I, and Addams makes the difficult decision to remain a pacifist.

1918 Addams gives talks for the Food Administration.

1919 Addams presides over the second congress of the Women's International League.

1920 Addams is blacklisted by the Lusk Report. The American Legion and the Daughters of the American Revolution also attack her as a Communist and Bolshevik.

1922 Addams publishes *Peace and Bread in Time of War*.

1929 At the sixth congress of the WIL in Prague, Addams resigns as president but is elected honorary president for life. Hull House celebrates its fortieth anniversary.

1930 Addams publishes the sequel to her autobiography, *The Second Twenty Years at Hull House*.

1931 Addams is awarded the Nobel Peace Prize.

1933 Addams serves on the Chicago advisory committee of the Housing Division of the Public Works Administration under the New Deal.

1935 Addams dies in Chicago on May 21, 1935.

Bibliography

Books

Addams, Jane. *Democracy and Social Ethics.* New York: Macmillan, 1902.

Addams, Jane. *The Excellent Becomes Permanent.* New York: Macmillan, 1932.

Addams, Jane. *The Long Road of a Woman's Memory.* New York: Macmillan, 1917.

Addams, Jane. *My Friend Julia Lathrop.* New York: Macmillan, 1935.

Addams, Jane. *A New Conscience and an Ancient Evil.* New York: Macmillan, 1912.

Addams, Jane. *Newer Ideals of Peace.* New York: Macmillan, 1907.

Addams, Jane. *Peace and Bread in Time of War.* New York: Macmillan, 1922.

Addams, Jane. *The Second Twenty Years at Hull House.* New York: Macmillan, 1930.

Addams, Jane. *The Spirit of Youth and City Streets.* New York: Macmillan, 1909.

Addams, Jane. *Twenty Years at Hull House.* New York: New American Library, 1981.

Addams, Jane, with Emily Balch and Alice Hamilton. *Women at the Hague: The International Congress and its Results.* New York: Macmillan, 1915.

Davis, Allen F. *American Heroine, The Life and Legend of Jane Addams.* New York: Oxford University Press, 1973.

Farrell, John C. *Beloved Lady: A History of Jane Addams' Ideas on Reform and Peace.* Baltimore: the Johns Hopkins Press, 1967.

Ginger, Ray. *Atgeld's America, The Lincoln Ideal Versus Changing Realities.* New York: Funk & Wagnalls Co., 1958.

Lasch, Christopher. *The Social Thought of Jane Addams.* New York: The Bobbs Merrill Co., 1965.

Linn, James Weber. *Jane Addams.* New York: Greenwood Publishers, 1968.

Meigs, Cornelia Lynde. *Jane Addams: Pioneer for Social Justice.* Boston: Little, Brown & Co., 1970.

Tims, Margaret. *Jane Addams of Hull House.* New York: Macmillan, 1961.

Wise, Winifred. *Jane Addams of Hull House.* New York: Harcourt, Brace, Jovanovich, 1935.

Selected Articles

Addams, Jane. "A Modern Lear." *Survey*, XXIV (November 2, 1912), pp. 131–137.

Addams, Jane. "The Subjective Necessity for Social Settlements" and "The Objective Value of a Social Settlement." *Philanthropy and Social Progress*. New York: Thomas Y. Crowell & Co., 1893, pp. 1–26, 27–58.

Conway, Jill. "Jane Addams: An American Heroine." *Daedalus*, XCII (Spring 1964), pp. 761–780.

Scott, Anne Firor. "Saint Jane and the Ward Boss." *American Heritage*, December 1960, pp. 12–17, 94–99.

Index

About the Author

L eslie Wheeler was born in California and majored in English and history at Stanford University. She received a master's degree in English from the University of California at Berkeley. She has co-authored textbooks in American history and has written two biographies and a number of magazine articles in the area of American history. She now lives in Cambridge, Massachusetts.